Praise for
THE KIDS' GUIDE TO
Working Out
CONFLICTS

"Naomi Drew's colorful and attractive *The Kids' Guide to Working Out Conflicts* builds on the experience of many of today's middle schoolers in turning ugly situations into opportunities for positive relationships."—Elise Boulding, Professor Emerita of Sociology, Dartmouth College, former Secretary General of the International Peace Research Association, and author of *Cultures of Peace*

"This book is a gold mine of wonderful strategies that will help today's youth become peaceful, contributing, healthy beings."—Michele Borba, Ed.D., author of *Don't Give Me That Attitude!* and *No More Misbehavin'*

"This book leaves readers with everyday strategies to work out conflicts, and, as a result, become happier in their relationships with their family and friends. Naomi Drew offers her readers the hope that every day is an opportunity to change."—Christopher J. Campisano, Ed.D., New Jersey Department of Education

"I heartily recommend *The Kids' Guide to Working Out Conflicts* to any parent or child—or world leader for that matter."—Greg Martin, coauthor of *The Buddha In Your Mirror*

THE KIDS' GUIDE TO

Working Out
CONFLICTS

How to Keep Cool, Stay Safe, and Get Along

NAOMI DREW, M.A.

free spirit
PUBLiSHiNG®

Works
for kids®

Library of Congress Cataloging-in-Publication Data
Drew, Naomi.
    The kids' guide to working out conflicts : how to keep cool, stay safe, and get along / Naomi Drew.
      p. cm.
    Summary: Describes common forms of conflict, the reasons behind conflicts, and various positive ways to deal with and defuse tough situations at school, at home, and in the community without getting physical.
    Includes bibliographical references and index.
    ISBN 1-57542-150-X
1. Interpersonal conflict—Juvenile literature. [1. Conflict management. 2. Conflict (Psychology) 3. Fighting (Psychology) 4. Interpersonal relations.] I. Title.
    BF637.I48D74 2004
    303.6'9'0835—dc22

2003021108

At the time of this book's publication, all facts and figures cited are the most current available; all telephone numbers, addresses, and Web site URLs are accurate and active; all publications, organizations, Web sites, and other resources exist as described in this book; and all have been verified as of February 2004. The author and Free Spirit Publishing make no warranty or guarantee concerning the information and materials given out by organizations or content found at Web sites, and we are not responsible for any changes that occur after this book's publication. If you find an error or believe that a resource listed here is not as described, please contact Free Spirit Publishing. Parents, teachers, and other adults: We strongly urge you to monitor children's use of the Internet.

The people depicted on the cover are models and are used for illustrative purposes only. The names of the young people quoted throughout the book have been changed to protect their privacy.

Edited by Marjorie Lisovskis
Cover and interior design by Marieka Heinlen
Index by Kay K. Schlembach
Illustrated by Chris Sharp

10 9 8 7 6 5 4 3 2 1
Printed in the United States of America

Free Spirit Publishing Inc.
217 Fifth Avenue North, Suite 200
Minneapolis, MN 55401-1299
(612) 338-2068
help4kids@freespirit.com
www.freespirit.com

The following are registered trademarks of Free Spirit Publishing Inc.:

FREE SPIRIT®
FREE SPIRIT PUBLISHING®
THE FREE SPIRITED CLASSROOM®
SELF-HELP FOR KIDS®
SELF-HELP FOR TEENS®
WORKS FOR KIDS®
HOW RUDE!™
LEARNING TO GET ALONG™
LAUGH & LEARN™

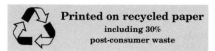

DEDICATION

This book is dedicated to every young person
who has ever extended a hand of kindness to kids who are
left out or picked on. May countless others follow in your footsteps.

ACKNOWLEDGMENTS

Books are never written alone. I'm grateful to so many people for their involvement. My warmest thanks to:

- my wonderful editor, Margie Lisovskis, for her warmth, insight, keen eye, and commitment to excellence.

- Free Spirit staffers, Douglas Fehlen, Darsi Dreyer, and Amy Dillahunt, for the generous support they have given to this book.

- Judy Galbraith for her enthusiasm, support, and belief in this book, and for her dedication to the well-being of kids.

- my husband, Mel Baum, for his ever-present faith in me and the work I do.

- my sons, Michael and Tim, whose lives continue to inspire me every day.

- my father, Philip Schreiber, for his support and belief in me.

- my mother, Molly Schreiber, may she rest in peace, for her luminous soul, and for setting the foundation for all the work I do.

- my dear friend, Virginia Abu Bakr, for her wisdom and loving support, and for the peace shield concept that appears in this book.

- my gifted teacher, Kirin Mishra, who provides the spirit of Saraswati that runs through my life.

- my guidance counselor and friend, Yvonne Amalina DeCarolis, for the information and insight she provided for this book.

- all the kids whose words and thoughts appear in this book. Your impact is far-reaching.

- all the kids I've worked with over the years whose voices speak through the words I write. You have taught me more than you will ever know.

- all the teachers, administrators, and counselors I have had the privilege to work with. Your concerns and insights flow through this book.

CONTENTS

LIST OF REPRODUCIBLE PAGES

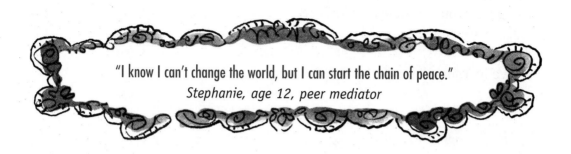

"I know I can't change the world, but I can start the chain of peace."
Stephanie, age 12, peer mediator

INTRODUCTION
How This Book Can Help You

"My brother is such a pain. Every single day he says or does things that make me want to scream. I tell him to stop, then I get in trouble!"

"Last year I hated going to school. There was this girl in my class who was always bugging me. We were always getting into arguments. I'd end up going home in a bad mood all the time."

"My mom's always on my case. We fight all the time. Sometimes I wish I could just move out!"

"A lot of boys in my class who want to look cool pick on people and get into fights to show off."

"Kids of different races are always picking on each other. Why does it have to be that way?"

Well, it *doesn't* have to!

The quotes you just read are from 10- to 15-year-olds who were surveyed or interviewed for this book. As you can see from their comments, if you sometimes have problems getting along with the people in your life, you're not alone. While writing the book, I surveyed more than 1,000 middle school students to find out how conflict impacts their lives. (You'll find the survey on pages 137–138.) I wanted to know what they get into conflicts over, how they respond to conflicts, and what kinds of things they want to learn about managing anger and dealing with conflicts. In addition to the survey, I talked with many kids face-to-face to hear their personal stories and feelings about conflicts they have at school and at home. Many of the students said they see or experience conflict every day, and they don't like it. Ninety percent of the students who answered the survey said they believe learning to solve conflicts is important.

Conflict is a major source of stress in many kids' lives. It's also the cause of violence in schools, homes, and the world at large. So many of us—adults as well as kids—go around feeling upset, annoyed, irritated, threatened, perturbed, or just plain mad because of conflicts that happen. Not knowing how to respond makes things even worse. If this is the case for you, then you've come to the right place. This book is filled with practical things you can do to get a handle on conflict and get along better with the people in your life.

The Truth About Conflict

Conflict is part of being human. It's normal and natural, and it happens when people have differing points of view or sets of needs. Your dad tells you to change your pants because they're too baggy or too tight; you think they're just right. Your buddy wants to play video games; you want to play ball. Your best friend wants to talk on the phone; you need to study for a test. The problem isn't the conflict itself; *it's how you deal with it.* Sure, it's annoying when someone disagrees with you or tells you to do what you don't want to do. But there's something really important to know:

> **When it comes to conflict, you always have a choice about how you're going to handle it. This means you have a lot of power, because what *you* choose to do can determine how the conflict will turn out.**

Lots of people choose negative ways of dealing with conflict—ways that are *un*helpful and usually harmful. They do things like argue, name-call, swear, make sarcastic remarks, use other forms of meanness, or fight with fists or weapons. All these things make a conflict worse. If you choose the negative route, you or the other person might end up walking away mad or physically hurting each other. You both might get in trouble or have bad feelings about each other for a long, long time. You might have bad feelings about yourself, too, if you hurt someone else when inside you know it's wrong.

You can choose to do something different—something better. There are actually proven ways for handling conflict that are positive and fair, ways that allow both people to feel okay in the end. That's what *The Kids' Guide to Working Out Conflicts* is about. It will help you unlock the power you have to work out conflicts in ways you feel good about. And if you do the things suggested here on a regular basis, you'll find yourself getting along better with the people in your life, feeling better about yourself, and gaining more respect.

Sound too good to be true? It's not.

I know this first-hand because I do these things in my own life. In fact, helping people learn how to work out problems peacefully has become my life's work. I learned about conflict resolution the hard way, though. When I was a kid, I was constantly fighting with my brothers, sisters, and parents, and sometimes with my friends. Until I found ways to deal with conflicts more peacefully, all that fighting made me unhappy. When I grew up and became a parent and a teacher, I promised myself that I would find ways to help my own kids and my students get along. So I began a search for strategies that worked, and even created a few of my own. Little by little, I saw my sons and my students getting along better and feeling better about themselves. I saw the number of conflicts they had decrease and their positive relationships multiply.

For many of these young people, the effects were long-term. One former student told me, "Our school taught me so much about conflict resolution and peacemaking. What I learned as a kid I've been able to apply in many other areas of my life, even in college." My two sons also learned this. They found out how to overcome their habit of fighting and ended up getting along really well with each other and with people in their lives. Now that they're adults, they're best friends and their lives are filled with strong relationships.

The bottom line is this: People can learn how to work out conflicts—and when they do, they're happier. You can be this kind of person. To learn how, you'll need three important things:

1. the desire to change

2. the willingness to try something new

3. patient determination, also known as *perseverance*

If you develop perseverance now, it will help you with everything in your life, not just resolving conflicts. It will also help you earn good grades, do better in sports or other activities, stay in shape, and become the kind of person you want to be. Anything worth achieving takes perseverance.

About This Book

Working Out Conflicts is divided into eight chapters, which I've called steps. Each step will help you increase your ability to be an effective conflict solver. You'll find out how to be respectful yet firm so you can stand up for yourself without making matters worse. You'll learn skills for listening, guidelines for talking out problems, strategies for managing anger and stress, ideas for staying safe, and ways to bring more peace to the wider world. Throughout the book you'll also find:

*   stories and scenarios—real-life examples of conflicts kids have had and ways they have solved them

*   quotes and facts from the students who completed the survey

*   simple activities that let you take a look at your own life to see how you can apply what you're reading about to everyday situations

*   self-tests, conflict logs, and other forms you can use to track your progress and explore new ideas

*   books, Web sites, and organizations where you can find more information on many of the topics in this book

You'll get more out of the book if you do as many of the activities as possible. Have a notebook handy as you read so you can complete the exercises, record your thoughts, and jot down notes. You don't have to show your private writing to anyone else—it's just for you. Whether you write a little or a lot, be sure to talk about and practice some of the exercises with other kids and adults. This way you'll build your confidence in dealing with other people. You'll also get better at communicating in ways that are brave, strong, respectful, and honest.

Please share *Working Out Conflicts* with the adults in your life—teachers, family members, counselors, and youth leaders. By doing this, you'll help them show even more kids how to work out conflicts, manage anger, and get along better. Just think: What if your whole school learned how to do this? What if your family learned, too? What could the world be like if more and more people knew how to solve conflicts and didn't resort to violence? *You* could be the start.

I'd love to hear from you about how this book helps you or about any questions you have. Here's where you can write to me:

c/o Free Spirit Publishing Inc.
217 Fifth Avenue North, Suite 200
Minneapolis, MN 55401-1299
Email: help4kids@freespirit.com

Enjoy this book, and remember: No matter how many conflicts you've had in the past . . . and no matter how many conflicts you see other people having . . . every day is an opportunity for change. The key to change is within you. I wish you peace. And I hope the book makes a very positive difference in your life.

Naomi Drew

Real words from the survey

"I most want to learn how to cope better with everyone and not hurt any feelings."

"I'd like to learn to talk to people who are fighting, because when they fight they don't solve anything."

"I most want to learn how to stop conflict."

STEP 1
Open Your Mind

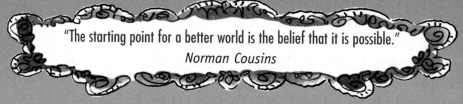

"The starting point for a better world is the belief that it is possible."
Norman Cousins

In this chapter you'll discover:

* why people have conflicts
* an important key to avoiding and stopping conflicts
* a way to start gaining control when it comes to conflict

It *is* possible to solve conflicts peacefully, and in this chapter you're going to start finding out how. A conflict is a fight, disagreement, or misunderstanding. Conflicts happen between people of all ages everywhere: in homes and schools, neighborhoods and communities, workplaces and playing fields, and places of worship. They happen between individuals, groups, and countries.

Sometimes conflicts happen inside our heads. You probably know all too well the kinds of inner conflicts young people face: Should you go to the party or the movies? Should you wear this outfit or that one? Should you respond to the mean remark the kid next to you made or just ignore it? Sometimes inner conflicts are really tough ones, like if your good friends have started smoking pot and they want you to join in. You know it's wrong, but you want to be part of the crowd. Big conflict. What do you do?

The choices you make when you have conflicts inside your head can lead to conflicts with other people. For instance, if you don't want to smoke pot, your friends might pressure you or make fun of you. Or maybe your friends are picking on someone; you know it's wrong and you want to speak up, but you're afraid if you do they'll pick on you, too. Conflicts like this can be hard, because while your head, heart, and conscience are telling you one thing, people around you are saying something else. That's the time to trust your instincts. They'll almost always guide you to do what's right.

What Starts a Conflict? What Makes It Grow?

Although there are lots of different causes for conflicts, they usually stem from people's needs and wants. For example, maybe you need your algebra book back right away, but your friend needs to keep it a little longer because she forgot hers again. Or you want to watch one TV show and your brother wants to watch another. Or you want to lie around for a while on a Saturday morning, but your mom needs you to help watch your little sister. When different needs or wants collide, conflict results. That's exactly what happened to Carla:

"My friend Mandy and I aren't speaking. It started the other day at lunch when Stacy came and sat with us. Usually it's just me and Mandy. But that day Mandy kept talking to Stacy and ignoring me. I felt totally left out, so I told Mandy I was going to the girls' room. When I came back, I figured I'd sit with someone else. Later when Mandy saw me in the hall, she started acting mean and accused me of ditching her! Now we haven't talked in three days."

What started this fight? Carla wanted to spend time alone with Mandy, but Mandy wanted to include Stacy. Their wants collided, feelings got hurt, and BOOM!— conflict.

Hurt feelings are a major cause of conflict. You've probably been in situations where someone says or does something, either accidentally or on purpose, that hurts your feelings. So you respond by saying something hurtful in return or talking behind the person's back. What happens next? The person reacts to what you do, and then . . . ? You've got it. Conflict.

The Survey Says

Boys' Top 5 List of Conflict Starters Between Friends

1. Who's right and who's wrong
2. Bragging
3. Who does better at sports or in school
4. The rules of games
5. Insults and name-calling

Girls' Top 5 List of Conflict Starters Between Friends

1. Gossip, rumors
2. Having secrets told
3. Boyfriends
4. Feeling jealous or left out
5. Mean remarks behind people's backs

Bad moods can lead to conflict, too. It's only human to feel cranky once in a while, and when that happens, you may find the people around you kind of annoying. As a result, conflicts can flare up. Thanh's story is a case in point:

"My mom is pretty okay, but sometimes she REALLY gets on my nerves. Like the other day, I was tired because I stayed up too late to study for a math test. When I came downstairs I was in a crummy mood and I just wanted to be left alone. Plus I didn't feel like eating. Sometimes I just can't eat first thing in the morning, but I always have something later at school.

"Mom knows that, too. But she kept bugging me about eating breakfast. Finally I yelled, 'Would you get off my case?!' I know if I'd been in a better mood, I wouldn't have shouted at her like that. But I did, and then she went through the roof. She started lecturing me about how disrespectful I was and if she heard one more fresh word out of my mouth she'd ground me for a week. And I said, 'Go ahead, I don't care!' and took off for the bus. She was fuming. And when I got home, I was grounded."

Talk About It

What are some other ways Thanh could have handled the situation with his mother? Talk this over with a friend or family member. How many better ideas can you come up with?

Thanh's grouchy mood helped to set off this conflict. He didn't think before he spoke because he was too upset inside. But what if Thanh hadn't let his bad mood lead him into this situation? Picture what might have happened if Thanh had backed off for a minute, taken a few deep breaths, calmed down, and then answered his mom differently. He might have said something like, "Mom, I know you're just trying to help, but right now I'm really not hungry. How about if I take a granola bar and juice to have during first period study hall?" His mom's reaction would have been entirely different.

Conflict Triggers

Needs and wants, hurt feelings, bad moods—all of these can *trigger* (set off) a conflict. What triggers your conflicts? Things people say? Looks they give? Unfairness? What role do your feelings play? In the survey, middle school kids described lots of different situations and feelings that triggered conflicts with friends and family members. Here are some of the things they wrote:

"Some people become jealous when I go somewhere with someone else instead of them. That'll start a conflict."

"Sometimes I get mad at my friend when he's talking a lot of junk."

"I get mad at my friends when they tell people my secrets or talk behind my back."

"My sister and brother antagonize me and then I call them names or insult them in some other way."

"My parents always give more credit to my brother and I get mad."

"I'm always fighting with my sister because she won't stay out of my life."

One way you can help yourself handle conflicts better is to understand what annoys or upsets you (that's your trigger) and what you can do instead of just reacting. Once you know what puts you into "conflict mode," you can be aware of it and stop yourself before you do something to make things worse. It's kind of like stopping yourself from catching a cold. If you understand what keeps your body strong—like eating right, getting enough rest, and exercising regularly—you can help prevent that cold by

Write About It

Make copies of the "My Conflict Triggers" form (page 19) and use it to learn more about what leads you into conflict. Over the next few days, notice the situations, people, and feelings that often trigger conflicts for you. Write about these on your form and see what you discover. Do similar things set you off? What feelings get triggered? Is there a better way you can deal with the people who tend to get on your nerves?

The Survey Says

Top 10 Conflict Starters at Home

1. Sharing possessions
2. Who started it
3. Phone time
4. Who gets more stuff from the store
5. Which TV shows to watch
6. Siblings in my room or space
7. Shower times
8. Chores
9. Food and drinks
10. Too much interrupting and ignoring

doing the things that work. It's the same with conflicts: Understanding what triggers your conflicts and knowing what works to calm you down can help prevent conflicts from getting out of control. The benefit? A happier life, and even a healthier one—because researchers have found that getting along with others keeps people healthier.

Right about now you may be thinking something like this:

"Yeah, right. Some people might be able to stop or fix conflicts, but they don't have to live with *my* sister . . . or listen to *my* teacher . . . or get along with *my* stepdad . . . or deal with the kids on *my* bus."

You're right. Working out conflicts isn't always easy. But it's always worth the effort. It's a lot like learning how to ride a bike. Remember the first time you rode without training wheels or someone's strong hand helping to keep you steady? You probably fell and scraped your legs plenty in the beginning. But after you practiced, you started coasting along more and more easily. That was *perseverance:* you kept trying and stuck with it till you could do it. Working out conflicts takes perseverance, too. Also courage. It can feel pretty risky to take the lead in dealing with conflict. Anything that requires us to change is a little scary at first, but we all have storehouses of courage inside ourselves that we've never even used. Flexing our courage muscles makes us stronger. Are you ready and willing to flex yours? If you are, you've already made a super-important choice. Here's why:

Willingness is the key to getting started.

Willingness Lets You Put the Brakes on Conflict

Think about that two-wheeler again. The thing that enabled you to learn how to ride it was your *willingness* to try. Without willingness, you'd still have training wheels. Working out conflicts is like that. If you're not truly willing to work things out, all the right words and techniques in the world aren't going to help. But if you're willing to try, and even willing to fail a few times, you'll be amazed at the results.

Sometimes people say they want to work out conflicts, but what they really want to do is keep on fighting. Take a look at this conversation I had with a boy named Jason:

"It's My Sister's Fault"

Jason: My little sister Marci drives me nuts. She's always coming in my room without knocking, and when I tell her to get out, she keeps bugging me and won't leave.

Me: Then what do you do?

Jason: I chase her, and she runs all over the place screaming.

Me: And then ...?

Jason: I catch her and wrestle her to the ground.

Me: What happens then?

Jason: Sometimes she starts to cry. Then my mother yells at me.

Me: And then you get punished?

Jason: *(angry)* Yeah, and it's not fair! It's all Marci's fault. She shouldn't keep coming in my room!

Me: Have you tried talking to her about it?

Jason: No. What good would that do?

Me: Maybe then you'd solve the problem.

Jason: Why should *I* try to solve it? *She* always starts it. Plus, I like chasing her and wrestling her down. It's fun!

Jason seems more interested in keeping the conflict going than in working it out—even though he often ends up in trouble. His *unwillingness* stands in his way. Like many people, Jason isn't willing to see or admit his role in keeping

Think About It

Are there times you want to keep a conflict going? Why? What happens? How do you feel?

The Survey Says

45% of students said they had conflicts one or more times each day.

What Do YOU Say?

- Do you have conflicts several times a day? At least once a day? Less than once a day?

- How would it feel to have fewer conflicts?

the conflict going. Jason is caught in this trap of getting into conflicts with his sister, and then getting punished. Before long, his mother is going to start blaming him every time there's a problem (if that isn't already happening). But by taking responsibility, Jason can free himself from this negative pattern.

Think about it. Sure, it's fun to tease your sister or brother once in a while, but isn't it more satisfying to get along with the people you live with and not always be in trouble? Also, isn't it nice to have the trust of the adults in your life? Once you lose trust, it's hard to get it back. But when you have it, you feel really good about yourself—and you have the chance to earn greater freedom, too.

What Happens When You're NOT Willing to Work Out Conflicts?

When you're unwilling to work out a conflict, three things usually happen:

1. Blame and more blame. Maybe you've heard of the "blame game": You blame someone for causing a problem. That person blames you back. No one takes responsibility and the conflict is never resolved. You can end up having the same conflict over and over again. And all this blaming hides an important truth: in most conflicts, BOTH people are responsible in some way. In Jason's case, his sister was responsible by going into his room without asking, but Jason was responsible because he chased her and wrestled her to the ground. How else do you think he could have handled the problem?

2. Escalation. When no one takes the lead in stopping the blame game, the conflict usually gets louder, meaner, and bigger. That's what *escalation* is. Angry words can lead to shouts, shoves, hits, punches, or worse. Sometimes what starts off as a simple little argument blows up into a gigantic mess where everyone gets in trouble and both people are hurt emotionally or physically.

3. More conflicts. The saddest thing that happens when people are unwilling to work things out is that they end up having conflicts all of the time, and life becomes even more stressful. Once this happens to you, everywhere you go, you'll run into someone you've either had a problem with or might have a problem with in the future. After a while, you'll start to feel like a magnet for conflicts. That's no fun!

What Are Your Willingness Blocks?

Willingness blocks are things that make you resist working stuff out. Take this quick self-test to see which blocks could be getting in your way:

I'd like to stop having conflicts, BUT sometimes (or often) . . .

✓ I want to be "right" and show that the other person's "wrong."

✓ I don't want to look weak.

✓ I feel like people will take advantage of me if I compromise.

✓ I like to be on top.

✓ I don't like the other person.

✓ I'm afraid of looking stupid.

✓ I feel too angry to deal calmly with the situation.

✓ I want to take things out on the other person.

✓ I want to get even for something the other person said or did.

✓ I don't know how to change. Fighting is the only way I've ever dealt with conflict.

Think About It

Think about someone you often have conflicts with. What are your willingness blocks with this person? What feelings seem to stop you from trying to work things out?

Do any of these statements fit for you? If so, join the club. We all experience one or more of these willingness blocks when conflicts arise. But we don't have to let them continue to stand in our way. Instead, each time you find yourself feeling or thinking something that will keep a conflict going, ask yourself two questions:

1. **Is it worth it to hold onto this block? AND**
2. **Am I willing to summon up the courage to change?**

Here's the problem: Holding onto willingness blocks practically *guarantees* that your conflicts aren't going to get worked out. And when you go around having conflicts all the time, lots of negative things happen. People begin to avoid you. They start to think of you as a troublemaker. You lose friends and feel lonely. You get punished and feel stressed. Soon you're feeling bad about yourself more and more of the time. Your overall health can be affected. And during all this, you're setting a lifetime pattern of dealing with conflicts in negative ways.

Does this have to happen to you? Absolutely not. You may want to blame or attack the other person, but you don't have to go down that path. You see, you have the power to prevent conflicts from escalating. Somebody has to take that first step, and that somebody can be you. Even if you think the other person is more responsible than you are, it's still worth trying to work out the problem.

The most mature and honest thing you can do is ask yourself how *you* might be responsible instead of just blaming the other person. Then take a step toward working things out. Soon you're going to find out exactly how to do this.

The Survey Says

10 Ways Kids React to Conflict

1. Fight, kick, punch, push
2. Argue, curse, call each other names
3. Give the silent treatment
4. Make threats
5. Spread rumors
6. Talk it out
7. Apologize
8. Go to a teacher or another adult
9. Walk away
10. Ignore it

What Do YOU Say?
How do you handle conflict? What works? What doesn't?

Yes, it can be hard to do, sometimes very hard. But it's worth it if you want to have stronger friendships, get along better at home and at school, and feel good about yourself. Plus you'll have the satisfaction of knowing that you flexed your courage muscle in a very important way.

What Happens When You ARE Willing to Work Out Conflicts?

Now for the good news: Even if only *one* person is willing to work out a conflict, it's still possible. Here's why. When you're willing to work things out, you act differently than when you're not. Your mind is open, and so are your ears. This means you can really listen to what the other person thinks and feels. And when you're willing to listen, very often the other person will listen, too. Does this work every time? Not 100

Try It

The next time you start having a conflict with a friend, a teacher, or someone at home, put your willingness blocks aside. Remind yourself that *you* can do something to ease the conflict. Instead of just trying to get *your* point across, listen. Even if you don't agree, try keeping your mind open for just a little while, and let the other person get the words out. Then ask the person to listen to you. Say what you have to say respectfully. Let your face and body language show the same respect that your words do. As you talk and listen, keep your mind open. Rather than thinking about how to get your way, think about how the problem might be solved.

Then see what happens. Did the problem get resolved? How do you feel about what you did?

percent, but you'd be surprised how often it does. Many times if you act mean toward someone, the person acts mean right back at you. But if you're at least willing to listen to what somebody has to say, she or he will start to calm down:

"Hey—That's Mine!"

Todd: Hey, that's my calculator!

Jamal: No it's not. It's *my* calculator.

Todd: *(starts to grab)* No it's not. It's mine. Give it to me now!

Jamal: Hold on a minute. I'm just gonna put the calculator back on the table. Let's talk about this. It's not worth getting in a fight over.

Todd: There's nothing to talk about. It's my calculator!

Jamal: Why do you think it's yours?

Todd: *(reaches for calculator)* Because it is.

Jamal: *(takes a breath and steadies his voice)* Let's be fair about this, okay? I have the exact same calculator and I just put it down for a minute to get a piece of paper. Why do you think it's yours?

Todd: Because I brought it from home. My dad bought it for me last night.

Jamal: Well, my brother gave me the same kind of calculator. Let's see if we can figure out whose it is. Does yours have black tape on the back?

Todd: No, it's brand new.

Jamal: Well mine does. Plus, I put my initials on it in permanent red marker.

Todd: *(looks at the calculator)* Huh . . . I guess this *is* yours. Then where's mine? *(looks under his notebook and books)* Oh, here it is.

Jamal: Wasn't worth a fight, was it.

Todd: Guess not. Sorry.

Jamal: Forget about it.

Fact

One of the most common reasons people lose jobs is their inability to get along with bosses and other people they work with. By learning how to work out conflicts now, you'll be getting great practice for being successful on the job.

Jamal's willingness to hear Todd out made all the difference. You can probably picture what might have happened if Jamal had grabbed the calculator back and kept arguing. But he didn't do that. Instead, he made a conscious choice to take the lead in solving the conflict. In doing so, Jamal avoided making an enemy, and might even have made a friend. He kept himself out of trouble with his teacher and felt good about himself for handling the situation with self-control and maturity. By opening his mind, Jamal enabled Todd to open his as well. And who knows, other kids in the class may have learned something from watching.

Basement or Balcony—Your Choice

I was leading a workshop for teachers and we were talking about conflicts—the ones we saw among our students and the ones we had ourselves. I'll always remember the words of one wise teacher. She said, "I realized that when I'm involved in a conflict and the other person is acting nasty, if I do that, too, it's like I'm going down to the basement inside myself. But if I choose to keep behaving with dignity and respect, then it's like I've gone to the balcony."

Where would you rather be—in the basement or on the balcony? Sometimes when people get us really mad, we automatically go down to the basement. We don't even think about it—we're just there. But the truth is, the balcony is available to us in every moment, and when we choose to go there, we feel better about ourselves and the conflict works out more smoothly.

Write About It

Recall a conflict you've had recently. What did the other person do? What did you do? Did you go to the basement or balcony? How did you feel? What happened?

Don't judge yourself too harshly if you found yourself in the basement. We've all spent plenty of time down there. Observing your own behavior starts you on the road to making new choices. If in your heart you're willing to take responsibility and open yourself to change, getting to the balcony will be easier than you might think.

How much time do you spend in the basement? If your answer is "lots," then know this—you've got a balcony inside yourself, too. Many of us don't even realize that it's there. Or we've visited it once or twice, but now we've forgotten about it.

Give this some thought: Can you remember a conflict you had when you went to the balcony instead of the basement? How did it feel to be on the balcony? For most people it feels really good—fantastic, actually. Because when we go to the highest part of ourselves we feel proud and grown-up, knowing that we didn't let something or someone get the better of us.

Now, think of a time when you went to the basement. How did you end up feeling?

It's a big difference and an important choice: balcony or basement? You have the power to choose the balcony each time you have a conflict. By opening your mind, by being willing to make this choice, you take the first step to becoming a conflict solver.

Real words from the survey

"I watch people be mean to each other. I've decided to be better than that."

Most of my conflicts are with: _____

They usually happen because: _____

_____

What this person does that bothers me most: _____

_____

When she/he does this, here's how I usually feel: _____

Then here's what I usually do: _____

_____

And then he/she does this: _____

_____

If my best friend were having this conflict, I would offer this advice: _____

_____

Next time a conflict with this person is possible, here's something I can do to
make the conflict better: _____

_____

I also have conflicts with: _____

They usually happen because: _____

_____

What this person does that bothers me most: _____

_____

When she/he does this, here's how I usually feel: _____

Then here's what I usually do: _____

_____

And then he/she does this: _____

_____

If my best friend were having this conflict, I would offer this advice: _____

_____

Next time a conflict with this person is possible, here's something I can do to
make the conflict better: _____

_____

Decide to Become a Conflict Solver

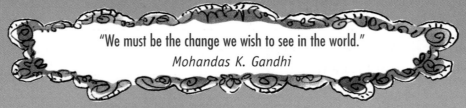

"We must be the change we wish to see in the world."
Mohandas K. Gandhi

In this chapter you'll discover:

- the difference between being a conflict solver and a conflict maker
- how to be a conflict solver with someone who's not willing to resolve conflicts
- how to be brave and strong without fighting
- answers to some of your important questions about resolving conflicts
- what to do when your friends are having conflicts

Even if you normally deal with conflict by using put-downs or shoves, you don't have to do this anymore. Every day is an opportunity to change. You have the power to get a handle on conflict so it doesn't have a hold on you. In fact, if you take control—if you decide to be a *conflict solver* rather than a *conflict maker*—your whole life could change for the better.

What Conflict Makers Do

Let's look at an example of a typical conflict between two kids. Ramón and Al were working on an art project. Things were going okay until Al left the paint jar close to the edge of the table. Then, when Ramón turned around, he knocked over the paint, splattering Al's pants and making a big mess on the floor. Here's what happened next:

"Oops!": Scene 1

Al: Watch out, idiot! Look what you just did!

Ramón: You're the idiot! If you hadn't moved the paint it wouldn't have gotten in my way!

Al: *(pushes Ramón)* Shut up, jerk!

Ramón: *(pushes back)* No, you shut up!

Teacher: What's going on here?"

Al and Ramón: *(point to each other)* He started it!

Teacher: That's enough! You both have detention after school today!

Sound familiar? This kind of stuff happens all the time. But conflicts don't have to end up the way this one did. When there's conflict, the choices *you* make in each moment can determine the outcome. This is often true even when the other person doesn't seem willing to cooperate.

In the scene you just read, Al and Ramón were being conflict makers instead of conflict solvers. They did some things that conflict makers tend to do: They reacted without thinking. They blamed the other person. They used put-downs. They got physical. They didn't think about how the other person might be feeling. They didn't look for solutions.

> ## The Survey Says
>
> 80% of students said they see kids having arguments or fights every day.
>
> **What Do YOU Say?**
> - How often do you see kids having arguments or fights?
> - How often do you have them yourself?

When people do these things, they give up their power by letting themselves react instead of *choosing* what to do next. Did you notice that when Al was nasty to Ramón, it triggered Ramón's nastiness? The negative energy grew—and the conflict escalated. Al became like an electrical charge that Ramón set off. Al called Ramón a name, then Ramón called Al a name. Al pushed, then Ramón pushed. By reacting without thinking, Ramón gave up control over his actions. Al kept reacting to Ramón as well. Each let the other person and his own bad feelings take control.

What Conflict Solvers Do

People really do have a choice about how conflicts turn out. Al, Ramón, you, and I all have this choice. The key is to act smart, not just react. This puts you back in charge as a conflict solver instead of a conflict maker.

Take a look at Al and Ramón's situation again. Let's see one way it might have turned out if Al had chosen to be a conflict solver:

"Oops!": Scene 2

Al: *(takes a deep breath, says silently to himself: "Cool it, Al. Relax before reacting"; now speaks to Ramón)* Whoa, Ramón, the paint . . .

Ramón: Oh, no! Why'd you have to move it?

Al: *(takes a deep breath, notices that Ramón feels bad about spilling)* I probably should've warned you. I got so involved in what we were doing I wasn't paying attention.

Ramón: *(thinks for a moment)* I guess I wasn't either. Sorry about your pants.

Al: We'd better get a sponge.

Ramón: There's one by the sink. I'll get it.

Al: I'll wipe up what's on the floor with paper towels.

Ramón: Whew, close call. Mr. Needham didn't even notice!

Totally different outcome. What made the difference?

You're right if you said it was Al's choice to take a step back and calm down before speaking. Also, Ramón's willingness to follow Al's lead and be kind rather than mean. Remember the choice you read about earlier—basement or balcony? In this situation, Al went to the balcony, and Ramón decided to climb up there with him. Instead of blaming and reacting, Al made instantaneous choices that actually helped solve the problem. One of them was putting himself in Ramón's shoes: He noticed how Ramón seemed to feel and imagined how he would have felt if he, Al, had been the one to spill the paint. And when Al was respectful, Ramón didn't get defensive—he didn't feel like he had to protect himself from put-downs or blame.

But what if Al hadn't been the one to take that first step back? How could Ramón have changed the outcome of the conflict?

"Oops!": Scene 3

Al: Watch out, idiot! Look what you just did!

Ramón: *(stops a moment, breathes deeply, says silently to himself: "Hold on, Ramón. You can handle this without losing your cool"; now speaks to Al)* Hey, Al, I didn't do it on purpose. Sorry about your pants, but I don't deserve to be called names.

Al: Well, you should have been more careful. Look what you did!

Ramón: Maybe I should have, but if the paint wasn't on the edge of the table, I probably wouldn't have knocked it over.

Al: Are you trying to blame me?

Ramón: *(takes another deep breath)* No, Al, but people make mistakes. Maybe we both did. Come on, why don't we clean it up together?

> Here Ramón is using a strategy called "Stop, Breathe, Chill." This strategy can be really helpful for calming down whenever you feel angry. You can read more about it in Step 5 on pages 70–75.

Ramón made his point without acting mean or resorting to name-calling. Even though Al was blaming him, Ramón didn't blame Al in return. He showed his strength in a different way. By taking a step back, breathing deeply, and making a calming statement, Ramón kept his cool and stood up for himself.

Put yourself in Ramón's place and take a slow, deep breath. Deep breathing is one of the most powerful tools for helping you keep your cool. It calms the body and feeds the brain. So even if your heart's pounding a mile a minute, deep breathing will actually make it pound a little slower. And as you feed oxygen to your brain, you'll help yourself think more clearly.

Calming statements help you take control, too. When you tell yourself, "Hey, I'm in charge here, and I can deal with this calmly," you create a steady, positive energy that helps you keep cool and act smart.

Try It

Pay attention to the things you tell yourself during difficult situations. Do you find yourself thinking negative thoughts, like "He's a jerk!" or "I'll show her!"? How do you feel when those angry thoughts bubble up? Try replacing the energy-zapping thoughts with calming ones that give you back your power: "Okay. I can deal with this." "I don't have to argue. I can stay cool." Notice how the calming thoughts affect your feelings.

Where Do You Stand?

You may have heard teachers or other kids talk about *conflict resolution*. This is another term for solving or resolving conflicts. When it comes to conflict resolution, where do you stand right now? What are you doing to be a conflict solver? Take this quick self-test to find out. Respond yes or no to each statement:

When I have a conflict . . .

✓ I try to calm down before I react.

✓ I do my best to avoid physical fighting.

✓ I believe I have more to gain by working things out.

✓ I listen to what the other person has to say.

✓ I try to see how I'm responsible instead of just blaming the other person.

✓ I look for ways to solve the problem rather than win the argument.

✓ I'm willing to compromise.

✓ I avoid using put-downs.

✓ I speak my truth, but I do it respectfully.

✓ I try to put myself in the other person's place instead of only focusing on my own stuff.

How many times did you answer yes?

- **Five or more?** If so, you're already a conflict solver a good part of the time. Keep at it! Also know that you'll become an even better conflict solver by working to turn your "no" answers into "yeses."

- **Fewer than five?** You're not there yet . . . but you can get there. Choose one new idea to try and do it until it starts to come more easily. Then choose another. Also continue doing whatever you said yes to.

- **If you answered yes to the third statement,** you've already made an important start. As you read earlier, being willing to work out conflicts is the first big step on the road to becoming a conflict solver.

One of the best ways to get a handle on the conflicts in your life is by observing yourself and noticing the kinds of conflicts you get into. The "Conflict Log" on page 35 will help you do this. Make seven copies of the page. Then, for the next week, take some time each day to answer the questions in the log. Every day, try to remember something you learned from your log that can help you take a step back and avoid or settle a conflict. At the end of the week, you'll have new insight into what gets you going and how you react. You'll probably notice ways you're becoming better at conflict solving.

When the Other Person Isn't Willing

It's never easy to be face-to-face with someone who's bent on winning and making you lose. You don't want to be a victim and let someone control you. And you know that fighting could make things worse. But it's possible to be strong AND be committed to resolving things peacefully. Sometimes this has to start with one person—the one who knows how to do it and is willing to try.

It's not just a choice between acting wimpy or bullying the other person. You can make your point and stick up for yourself without going on the attack. How? By choosing the path of courage, firmness, and dignity (pride and self-respect). That's what Lyla did when Jen confronted her in the hall at school:

"I Hear You've Been Talking": Scene 1

Jen: *(very angry)* Hey, loser, I hear you've been talking behind my back.

Lyla: *(feels scared, but takes a deep breath and thinks to herself: "I am calm and strong"; now speaks to Jen)* I'd appreciate it if you could tell me what happened without calling me names.

Jen: Why should I, when you went around telling people that I like Kevin?!

Lyla: *(takes another breath, repeats her calming statement to herself, then speaks)* Someone told you I said that?

Jen: Yeah! A few people did. You have no right to be talking about my business!

Lyla: *(breathes deeply again)* I'm sorry if people told you that, but that's not what I said.

Jen: Not according to them! Now the whole school thinks I want to go out with Kevin. I should kick your butt.

Lyla: *(breathes deeply, silently repeats her calming statement, then speaks to Jen)* I'm sorry people are gossiping, but would you like to hear what really happened?

Jen: Yeah, what?

Lyla: I told someone I saw you sitting next to Kevin at the basketball game and you were talking to each other. But I never said you liked him.

Jen: No way I like him! And you have no right talking about who I sit next to!

Lyla: *(stands tall and looks Jen directly in the eyes)* I didn't mean any harm, and I'm sorry this whole rumor started. Will you accept my apology?

Jen: *(calming down)* Maybe. Just don't go sticking your nose in my business.

Lyla: *(speaks firmly, sincerely, and with dignity)* I promise you, it'll never happen again. *(turns and walks away with her head held high)*

Real words from the survey

"Most of the time we have fights because someone is talking about another person."

"I have conflicts because of rumors and lies. Things get all messed up and everyone is mad at each other."

Jen was hurt and angry. She wanted to prove Lyla wrong, maybe even start a fight. But Lyla was willing to take the lead as a conflict solver. Lyla acted in a mature way. She understood that her words weren't the only things that were important. She didn't roll her eyes at Jen or use a sarcastic voice. When the discussion was over, she didn't go off in a huff—she simply walked away strong and tall. Instead of looking scared, she showed dignity. Lyla definitely didn't act like a victim, nor did she get pulled into a war of words or fists. Her words and actions showed self-confidence and self-respect. They also showed respect for Jen.

Fake It Till You Make It

It probably wasn't easy for Lyla to show so much courage. If you feel scared in a situation like this, it's really important to "fake it till you make it." In other words, act brave and strong even if you don't feel that way. When you do this, you send a message to your brain that you are brave and strong, and before long, you'll actually start believing it. Lyla felt scared when Jen confronted her, but she remembered to use deep breathing and a calming statement. She kept control and was able to act as if she wasn't afraid and speak the words she needed to speak.

Now imagine how this same conflict might have turned out if Lyla had let her own reactions be triggered by Jen's words:

"I Hear You've Been Talking": Scene 2

Jen: Hey, loser, I hear you've been talking behind my back.

Lyla: Who are you calling loser?

Jen: You! What're you gonna do about it?

Lyla: *(pushes)* That's what, loser!

Jen: *(pushes back)* I'm gonna kick your butt!

Lyla: *(pushes harder)* Oh yeah? I'm gonna kick yours!

Kids in the hall: FIGHT!!

You get the idea. When people react and let their emotions rule, they can end up creating conflicts. Resolving conflicts takes a cool head and a commitment to being respectful, honest, and fair. Doing this makes life better for you and the people around you, bringing a small dose of peace to the world. This happens each time you choose to work out conflicts rather than fight.

Team Earth Needs Your Help

It can seem so much easier to fight and blame—and that's what too many people do. (I don't have to tell you that, right?) But this is exactly why the world is in the shape it's in. Too much anger, too many put-downs, too much fighting, too much cruelty. Put all that stuff together and it's like a giant snowball covered with rocks and dirt rolling down a hill and picking up speed as it goes along. The result is more and more violence everywhere—at school, in homes, on the bus, in the streets, and throughout the world.

But *you* can be part of the solution. Even though you're only one person, you can make a difference in the world. How? By recognizing this important truth:

Every person counts.

Think about it: The world is made up of one person ... and one person ... and one person ... all added together. It's like in sports. You take one person and one person and one person, put them on a playing field, give them a common goal, and you've got a team. In order for that team to succeed, every person has to work together. That's why it's called teamwork.

But the largest team of all, Team Earth, is suffering from a lack of teamwork. Too many of us have forgotten that in order to meet the goal of living together peacefully, we have to find ways to cooperate and get along in spite of our differences.

Meeting that goal starts with you. You, sitting there with this book in your hands—Team Earth needs *you* to be a player in the game called peace. How you handle your conflicts at home, in the cafeteria, at the mall, in the gym, and in the schoolyard makes a difference in whether Team Earth will win the game of peace. If every one of us learns how to work out conflicts nonviolently from the time we're young, we can be a part of changing the world. Who knows, maybe you'll be a world leader someday. And even if you end up working at something else, what you're learning today will enable you to help the world be a lot more peaceful than it is right now. By choosing to become a conflict solver, you also become a peacemaker, something our world really needs.

"Yes, But" Questions

"Yes, but what about all the people who don't seem to care about Team Earth being peaceful?" Well, some of them will keep doing what they do—acting mean, using put-downs, fighting, cursing, leaving people out, using violence. But *you* can still make the choice to be respectful and caring. And if you do, you will eventually gain the respect of people around you. More than that, you'll respect yourself for standing out above the crowd and having the courage to be kind.

"Yes, but I don't want to look weak and have people make fun of me. Does being a peacemaker mean I have to let people walk all over me?" Definitely not. Remember, *mean* does NOT equal *strong*. In fact, the people who act meanest are often scared inside. They try to cut down others so they can feel bigger and more powerful. You won't come across as weak if you stand tall, look the person square in the eye, and speak from a place inside where you believe in yourself. Take a look at how Andi does this:

> **Real words from the survey**
>
> "Sometimes the brave kids just walk away. Sometimes the *un*brave kids fight and try to show off."

"Whose Shirt Is That?"

Jaquie: Whose shirt is that—your five-year-old sister's?

Andi: *(looks Jaquie in the eye and stands tall)* I guess you don't like it.

Jaquie: No way! It's lame.

Andi: *(continues to stand tall)* Well, I like it, and I don't think your comment is funny. *(turns and walks away confidently)*

Jaquie: *(calls to Andi)* Probably not, with your taste in clothes!

Andi: *(keeps walking with head high)* I'm happy with my taste.

Andi shows Jaquie and other people around her that Jaquie's mean words don't have any power over her. Even if Jaquie's remarks hurt Andi inside, she can keep her dignity and feel proud of herself.

You can, too. Just speak your words with strength and believe in what you say. Then let the rest go, even if you don't have the last word.

Dr. Martin Luther King Jr. was a peacemaker, and he was one of the strongest, bravest people who ever lived. He saw how violence leads to more violence. Dr. King believed in changing the world *nonviolently*, and he dedicated his life to that. He talked about violence as a kind of downward spiral that just keeps growing larger and larger and larger as it spins down and down and down.

Dr. Martin Luther King Jr.

You can avoid that kind of spiral in your life by choosing to become a conflict solver, a peacemaker. Like Dr. King, you can bring your own message of strength and dignity. You can lead yourself—and others—to the balcony instead of letting yourself be pulled down.

"Yes, but I've tried doing this conflict resolution stuff and it didn't work. Why should I try again?" Because by not doing it, you're part of the problem. Taking part in fighting, put-downs, and other forms of meanness will just keep those things going. Choosing to respond with courage and respect makes you part of the solution.

Sometimes conflict resolution takes time to work. It's just like when you learned to read. It didn't happen the first time you saw words on the page. You learned it slowly, and it took practice. Be patient and keep trying to solve conflicts. Trust that if you give it your best effort, it'll start to work. And if you try everything and the other person still won't cooperate, be proud of yourself because you had the courage to try.

"Yes, but my mom told me I should hit back if someone hits me. What's the right thing to do?" Your mom wants to protect you and she believes that this is the best way to do it. In most situations, you'll keep yourself a lot safer by doing the things you read about in this book. You know that conflicts can escalate. One or two punches usually lead to more punches, and harder ones. People become angrier and angrier, and they get hurt. Fighting can lead to more and more dangerous violence, too, where people start using weapons like knives and guns. That's another reason to resist the urge to fight whenever you can.

"Yes, but when I'm mad I don't want to try to work things out—I want to hurt the other person. Why shouldn't I?" Lots of people actually feel that way. Ask yourself *why* you would want to hurt another person. Is it because that person usually is mean to you? Acting mean back won't make things better for either of you. Or does someone else treat you badly and you want to take it out on other people? But how will hurting someone

Facts

In a national study of middle and high school students:

- Almost half of the students said that someone hurt them physically as a result of mean words.
- Two-thirds of the students said they had been teased or gossiped about in a mean way during the past month.

else help your situation? Or maybe you think it's just cool to act mean. The truth is, acting mean is *never* cool. Sure, sometimes you may admire someone who says or does something unkind that seems smart or funny. But when you act mean and hurt others, how do you feel inside? If you're like most kids, in the moment you might feel more powerful, or even glad you did it. But another part of you might feel really bad. By acting mean, you stand in the way of becoming your best self.

Meanness is a form of violence. You don't have to physically harm people to do violence to them. Cruel remarks, name-calling, gossiping, angry scowls, a roll of the eyes, shutting people out—these can all do damage. And they can lead to kicks and punches, too. So often kids tell me they've gotten into fights because someone looked at them funny.

Meanness is like a magnet that attracts more meanness to itself. But kindness and respect are magnets, too. Which kind of magnet would you rather have working for you?

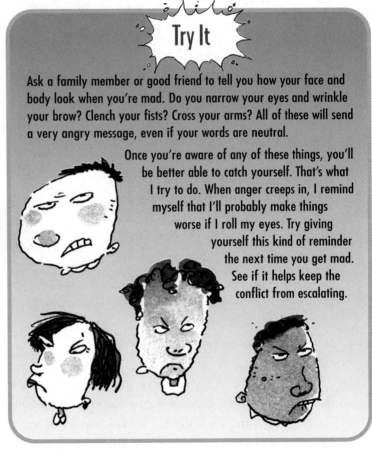

Try It

Ask a family member or good friend to tell you how your face and body look when you're mad. Do you narrow your eyes and wrinkle your brow? Clench your fists? Cross your arms? All of these will send a very angry message, even if your words are neutral.

Once you're aware of any of these things, you'll be better able to catch yourself. That's what I try to do. When anger creeps in, I remind myself that I'll probably make things worse if I roll my eyes. Try giving yourself this kind of reminder the next time you get mad. See if it helps keep the conflict from escalating.

"Yes, but what if I've tried talking things out and the person won't listen?" Sit down together at a neutral time—a time when neither of you is mad. Tell the person how you feel and see if she or he will listen.

That's what Raoul decided to do. He and Peter were assigned to the same social studies group. Raoul felt annoyed because Peter often tried to get everyone to do things his way. Raoul tried to talk to Peter about this, but it didn't help. Raoul knew that he and Peter were going to have to keep working together, so something had to change. He thought about it at home one night and decided to try to talk things over with Peter at lunch the next day.

"I Didn't Know You Felt That Way"

Raoul: Listen, Peter, I have something on my mind that I'd like to talk to you about.

Peter: What?

Raoul: I've been really uncomfortable about some things that have been happening in our social studies group.

Peter: What do you mean?

Raoul: I feel like you kind of take over and don't listen to other people's ideas.

Peter: I'm just trying to help us get organized. Sometimes we're all over the place.

Raoul: Yeah, but other people have things to say, too.

Peter: What do you mean?

Raoul: Sometimes when I try to talk to you, you roll your eyes or shake your head and don't listen. Then I feel like what I'm saying is stupid.

Peter: I didn't know you felt that way.

By deciding to try to solve the problem instead of complaining, using put-downs, or walking around angry, Raoul kept his own dignity *and* was able to start working toward a solution. He was proud of the way he handled the situation. He also saw that when he was direct and respectful, Peter wasn't defensive. Now Raoul felt more confident that he'd be able to handle other conflicts in a positive way. As a bonus, by working together with Peter, he might start to build a more positive relationship with him.

When you talk over the problem, listen to what the person is upset about. Do this with a calm expression on your face and without interrupting. Once you've listened respectfully, ask the person to listen to you. As you talk, avoid blaming, even if the person has been giving you a hard time. By not blaming, you'll open the door that allows the person to hear what you have to say. Be willing to take responsibility for your part. That's really important, because if you are, the other person might be, too. After you've talked things over, see if you can come up with some agreements to prevent future conflicts.

If you try this and the other person isn't willing to sit down with you, you can ask a teacher, coach, counselor, religious leader, family member, or another adult to help. In the next two chapters, you'll learn some skills you can use to talk through a problem—skills for listening, speaking, and coming to agreements.

> **Real words from the survey**
>
> "I had been picked on by a girl. I asked her why she was picking on me and she didn't have a reason. We started talking and eventually became good friends."

What to Do When Your Friends Have Conflicts

Lots of kids who talked to me or filled out the survey expressed concern about friends' conflicts. Maybe you're also someone who wants to make things better for your friends, but you don't know how. Here are some things you can do:

Try not to take sides. This is especially important if you feel caught between two people who are both close friends of yours. One or both friends may ask you for advice, or feel they really need your help. Be willing to listen, but let them know you care about both of them and need to stay neutral rather than take sides. Remind them that you like them both and encourage them to talk to each other. Say something like, "I really feel bad that you two are mad at each other, but I want to be fair and not take sides. Would you try talking to each other so you can work out the problem together?"

> **Real words from the survey**
>
> "When I see my friends fight, it's depressing."
>
> "It makes me uncomfortable because it's hard to tell when to get involved and when to leave the situation alone."

Don't get involved in gossip. If one friend starts talking about the other to you or to different people, don't join in. You can say something like, "I know you're mad at J.B. now, but it would probably be better if you tried discussing this with him face-to-face. Talking about him to other people could just make things worse." It's a good rule of thumb to always avoid discussing your friends' problem with other kids. Even though you mean well, this can still be seen as gossiping. If someone asks you about the conflict, you could say, "I'm not comfortable talking about it. I think they need to work it out between themselves."

Put yourself in their place. Imagine you were the one involved in the conflict and think about what would help you resolve it. Then, if your friends ask for advice, tell them your idea. Do this *only* if they ask for your opinion, though. Otherwise, don't try to fix the problem yourself.

Check Into It

What does your school do to help kids prevent and solve conflicts? Find out. Ask a teacher or counselor, or check at the school office. Could more be done? Talk to a counselor or teacher about starting a conflict resolution or peer mediation program at your school if you don't already have one. Consider becoming a peer mediator yourself! The world needs more people who are willing to resolve conflicts peacefully.

Suggest mediation. *Mediation* is a way of helping solve a disagreement. A mediator helps people work out the problem without getting in the middle of it. This person listens with an open mind, asks questions, and guides the people to resolve their conflicts fairly and respectfully. If your friends are having trouble solving their problem, you could suggest that they talk to a guidance counselor or teacher who can mediate. Or maybe your school has a *peer mediation* program where kids are trained to help other kids resolve their conflicts.

Real words from the survey

"It's up to each kid to decide on the person they want to be."

Are You Ready to Be a Conflict Solver?

You are a valuable member of Team Earth. By becoming a conflict solver, you'll not only change *your* life, you'll affect the lives of the people around you. Opening your mind is the first step. Making the decision to learn and practice ways to resolve problems peacefully is the second one. Are you willing to make this choice? I hope so, because you will improve your own life and help Team Earth move a little closer toward peace. Be patient with yourself and congratulate yourself for each step you take.

Date: _____

Here's who I had a conflict with: _____

What triggered it? _____

_____

How did I react? _____

_____

Did my actions make the conflict better or worse? _____

_____

How did the conflict end? _____

_____

Did I go to the basement? The balcony? A little of both? _____

_____

Here's how I feel about the way things turned out: _____

_____

_____

If my best friend had the same conflict, what would I have told him or her
to do? _____

_____

What could I have done differently? _____

_____

_____

When could I have stopped and taken some breaths to regain control? _____

_____

_____

What could I have told myself in order to calm down? _____

_____

_____

What is one thing I did today, or can do tomorrow, to help me stay calm and
in control during a conflict? _____

_____

Become a Better Listener

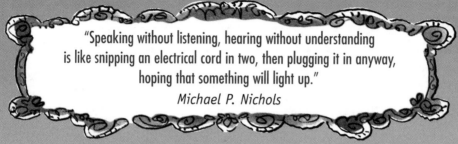

*"Speaking without listening, hearing without understanding
is like snipping an electrical cord in two, then plugging it in anyway,
hoping that something will light up."*
Michael P. Nichols

In this chapter you'll discover:

*   **why listening is important for preventing and solving conflicts**
*   **how to improve your listening**
*   **things you can do with your friends to help you all listen better**
*   **how you can use listening to resolve conflicts**

Listening is the most basic way we show respect for others, and the inability or unwillingness to listen is one of the biggest blocks to resolving conflicts. Many kids I spoke to or surveyed talked about how it felt when someone else didn't listen, saying things like this:

> "My mom always thinks she has all the answers. She never listens to what I have to say."
>
> "The kid who sits next to me in class really gets on my nerves. Every time I say anything he disagrees with he cuts me right off and talks over my voice. I can't stand it!"

You've probably been in situations where someone didn't listen to you. Maybe, too, you've noticed times when you didn't listen to someone else, or other people have told you that you don't always listen. Most of us have had both experiences—not being listened to, and not listening to others.

36

NOT Listening Fuels Conflicts

It's frustrating to be in both positions, and that's why conflicts can get started by poor listening on either person's part. When we don't listen, the person speaking feels disrespected. And someone who feels disrespected usually responds in a disrespectful way. The disrespectful words and actions just keep going back and forth, and the conflict keeps escalating.

When people don't listen to each other, conflicts can also go "underground": Suppose your buddy gets upset with you and tries to make a point, but you refuse to listen. Maybe your friend isn't the yelling and cursing type. Instead, he or she might just get quiet and give up on the conversation. Your friend stays mad and feels even madder than before, but tries to shove the feelings down inside and forget about them. This might seem okay for you, because the angry words are gone. The problem is, your friend's feelings don't disappear, and the conflict isn't solved. So later, or the next day, or even the next week, something happens and the person explodes at you. You might make a casual remark that rubs your friend the wrong way, and BOOM!—conflict. Or maybe the person decides not to be your friend anymore, or to talk behind your back. The conflict may have gone underground, but it sure didn't go away.

Think About It

- Think about a time when someone you were talking to wasn't listening. How did you feel?

- Why did you want the person to listen to you?

- Can you think of a time when *you* didn't listen to someone? What happened? How would your listening have helped the situation?

Listening Is Your Path to Personal Power

Listening, on the other hand—*really* listening—helps conflicts get better. When you listen to other people, they feel like you care about what they have to say. Also, you start to understand them better. And any information and understanding you gain can help you solve the conflict. Most important, when you listen to other people, they'll be more likely to listen to you.

Think about the people in your life. When someone's willing to hear you out and you're willing to hear that person out as well, you can actually start solving the problem. Without listening, this would be impossible.

Good listeners get along better with other people. They have fewer conflicts and are better able to deal with conflicts when they *do* have them. And here's more good news: Listening can be learned. It's a skill you can practice and master. If you do the things this chapter recommends, you will improve your listening and your life, and you'll handle conflicts a lot better. Then you'll be on your path to personal power. Personal power *doesn't* mean you have control over others. It means you have the power to be your best self.

With personal power . . .

- **You feel confident** about dealing with problems, handling unfamiliar situations, and learning new things.

- **You have compassion** toward other people, with a greater understanding of how they feel and what they want and need.

- **You respect yourself,** because you like the person you are. You know that feeling good about yourself means helping other people feel good, too.

- **You have the courage** to stand up for what's right. Other people don't have power over you—what you need is inside of yourself.

- **You gain other benefits as well,** including more friends, increased success in school, more respect from people, greater ability to work out conflicts, and stronger relationships.

Does personal power sound good to you? Then read on. You are about to discover the secrets of how to listen effectively—a key element of personal power.

Check Out Your Listening

How's your listening? Use this quiz for a quick self-check. Answer yes or no to each statement:

In a conversation . . .

✔ I make eye contact with the person who is speaking.

✔ I wait until the person is finished before I start talking.

✔ I focus on what the speaker is saying instead of just thinking about what I'm going to say next.

✔ I hear the speaker out even if I don't agree with what I'm hearing.

✔ I don't hijack the conversation and make it about me.

✔ I care about what the person has to say.

✔ I try to understand what the person believes, feels, and wants.

✔ If there's a conflict, I listen to the person's side of the story.

✔ I think it's important for people to listen to each other.

If you answered yes to at least four of these questions, you have some good listening skills already. If not, take heart! You're not the only person who needs to work on listening skills. No matter how you answered, you can build more personal power and become a stronger conflict solver by learning the secrets of effective listening and then practicing what you've learned. All it takes is deciding to begin and the willingness to keep trying even when you fall back into old patterns. (This happens to most people when they

Write About It

Listening helps people understand each other. Can you think of a time when you listened and understood someone better as a result? Or when someone listened to you and seemed to understand you more clearly because of it? What did you or the other person learn? How did it help you get along better?

first start learning a new skill.) It's worth the time to learn how to be a better listener. Once you do learn, you'll know how to do it for the rest of your life.

Take a look at how 13-year-old Lara succeeded in becoming a better listener:

"People used to always get annoyed with me, and I couldn't figure out why. One day it happened again—the kid who sat next to me got mad all of a sudden. So I got up the courage to ask him why. He said, 'Every time I talk, you cut me off and start talking about what *you* want to talk about. You don't seem to care about what I have to say at all.'

"He was right. I always wanted to talk and didn't have the patience to listen to anyone else. The truth hurt, but I needed to hear it. At home I started noticing how often I'd jump in and cut people off. It was hard for me not to do it, because it was what I'd always done. No wonder people were getting mad at me.

"I wanted to change, but I didn't know how, so I started thinking about who were really good listeners. Saj, this kid in my class, always listened like he really cared about what you were saying. It always felt good to be around him.

"I started paying more attention to what Saj did so I could learn from him. I noticed he was really patient—he never interrupted and he always looked right at you when you talked to him, like you were the only person there. His eyes never went over your head or around the room. So I started doing what he did.

"It took a lot of practice, but I'm doing a lot better now, and people don't get annoyed with me so much anymore. It feels really good. I like myself more now."

Think About It

- Think about someone you know who is a great listener. How do you feel when you're with this person?

- What do you notice this person does when listening to someone?

- What does the person do that you can try in order to become a better listener?

Lara did some very important things that helped her become a better listener:

- She had the courage to ask her classmate why he was mad at her and she didn't get defensive when he told her the truth.

- She made a commitment to work on improving her listening.

- She identified someone to use as a role model for good listening, watched him, and started imitating his good listening skills.

- She stuck with it, even when it was hard to do.

Try the Bad Listening/Good Listening Game

Here is a game you can play with two friends to help yourselves improve your listening skills. Ask one friend if the two of you can role-play for the other friend what really bad listening looks like. You play the bad listener and have your role-play partner be the person who's doing the talking.

Part 1: Bad Listening

Ask your fellow role player: "Where is your favorite place to go? Tell me about it."

As the person speaks, listen badly:

- Don't pay attention—look around the room instead.

- Interrupt.

- Change the subject.

- Avoid making eye contact.

- Act disinterested.

- Cross your arms and legs so you look like you'd rather not be listening at all.

- Turn your body slightly away from the speaker.

- Fidget.

- Ask about things the person already said: "Where'd you say you went?"

- Think about what *you* are going to say next.

- Play with your hair or move around in your chair.

- Touch things around you.

After a few minutes, ask the friend who's watching the role play to list all the things you did to listen badly. See how many the person can come up with.

Part 2: Good Listening

Switch places with the person who was watching. You take the role of observer. The new listener asks the other player the same question you asked before. But this time, the point is to role-play lots of ways to be a good listener:

- Look at the person who is speaking and keep good eye contact.

- Lean in toward the speaker and nod to show that you're interested and that you're following what the person says.

- Think about what the speaker is saying.

- Don't interrupt.

- Stay focused on the speaker and don't let yourself be distracted.

- Ask questions to make sure you understand what the speaker means.

- Act like the speaker is the only person in the room.

After a few minutes, tell the person who played the role of listener all of the things you saw him or her do to listen well. See how many there were.

Finally, ask the speaker how different it felt to be with someone who listened badly versus someone who listened well. Let the person describe what the experience was like in each role play.

Listen So You Really Understand: Reflective Listening

Asking helpful questions is an important part of good listening. To do this, you can use a unique approach called *reflective listening*. With reflective listening, you say back (reflect) what you heard the other person saying. This doesn't mean you repeat word for word exactly what the speaker said. (As you probably know, that can be pretty annoying.) Instead, paraphrase (use different words) to let the person know what you think she or he means. Sometimes it's helpful to start with the words "Sounds like" or to ask a question or use a questioning voice. Here's an example:

"Feeling Stressed?"

Marcus: I'm having so much trouble with math. Pre-algebra is so hard. I get really mixed up with all the letters and numbers together. I wish we'd go back to geometry.

Kylie: Sounds like you're really having a rough time with algebra. You're feeling stressed about it?

Marcus: Totally!

See what I mean? Kylie didn't repeat every word that her friend said. Instead, she used her own words to show that she heard what Marcus said and understood how he felt. That's what reflective listening is about. It gives you a way to let the person know you're listening and also lets you check to be sure that you've understood correctly. Here's another example:

"You Sound Excited"

Sam: So, what are you gonna do this weekend?

Lashanda: Well, there's a scout overnight on Friday and then on Saturday there's a big soccer game. And Sunday we're going to my aunt's house for a birthday party. I'll get to see my cousin!

Sam: Seems like you have a lot of great stuff going on—sleepover, soccer, party. You sound excited.

Lashanda: I am! Some weekends are boring.

Talk About It

Brainstorm some other reflective listening responses Sam and Kylie could have used. Try starting with phrases like these:

- "It sounds as if . . ."
- "It seems like . . ."
- "So you feel . . .?"

Did you notice how both Kylie and Sam picked up on the way their friends felt? That's an important part of reflective listening. It's not that you have to be a mind reader, but by paying careful attention and tuning in, you can learn a lot.

By the way, reflective listening can work really well with adults at home, especially when they're mad. Take a look:

"How Ya Doing?": Scene 1

Jeff: Hi, Mom. How ya doing?

Mom: I walk in the door and I trip over your book bag. Then I see your shoes and jacket in the middle of the floor. How do you think I'm doing?

Jeff: You're annoyed that I left my stuff all over. Sorry—especially about that book bag.

Mom: *(stops, notices she didn't get an excuse or argument, and speaks more calmly)* Apology accepted. But yes, I'm annoyed. Could you please put this stuff away now?

Jeff: Okay, Mom. I know how much you hate when I leave every-thing out.

Mom: *(smiles)* What's gotten into you?

As you can see here, when you listen this way, it can prevent a conflict from happening. Plus, it shows the other person you care. That is especially helpful if the other person is in a grouchy mood to begin with. Let's take a look at how this scenario might have gone if Jeff hadn't used any good listening skills but instead just reacted:

"How Ya Doing?": Scene 2

Jeff: Hi, Mom. How ya doing?

Mom: I walk in the door and I trip over your book bag. Then I see your shoes and jacket in the middle of the floor. How do you think I'm doing?

Jeff: Quit bugging me. You're barely in the door and you're on my case already.

Mom: *(raises her voice)* Watch your mouth, young man!

Jeff: Why should I? You're always on me about something!

Mom: *(louder)* Well if you'd just do what I ask, I wouldn't have to bug you! Do you think it's easy coming home after a full day of work and walking into a mess?

Jeff: *(yells)* You always make such a big deal of everything. All you ever do is yell!

Mom: That's it! Go to your room. You're grounded!

One way you can avoid scenarios like this is by taking a step back, breathing deep, and remembering to simply listen and try to understand the other person's point of view. Doing this might not guarantee that the person will calm down right away or let you off the hook if you've done something wrong. But you'll probably get a better result than by *not* listening.

Watch your facial expressions and tone of voice when you use reflective listening. If you use sarcasm, speak harshly, scowl, or roll your eyes, the other person can become more upset. The strongest message of your words is the way you say and present them.

When you first start using reflective listening, other people might not trust or understand what you're doing. But if you're really sincere about trying to understand the other person, the message will come through and people will start to notice. So stick with it.

Write About It

Next time you have a conflict, take time soon after to answer these questions in your notebook:

- What started the conflict?
- Was there a way I made it worse?
- How might the other person have been feeling?
- How would it have helped if I had been a better listener?
- What could I have said or done to listen better?

Play the "Sounds Like ..." Game

Here's another fun game to help you focus when you listen. It takes two people to play. In this game, you and your partner take turns asking each other some questions. (Ideas for questions to ask are below.) One person, the listener, asks a question first. The other person, the speaker, answers. When the speaker answers the question, it's the listener's job to listen with full concentration, and then say back two things:

- the main idea of what the speaker said

- the feelings the speaker expressed in words or seemed to be feeling

Here are some examples:

Questions to ask:
- Could you tell me about your favorite things to do when you have free time?
- Could you describe your earliest memory?
- If you could be anything you wanted, what would you be and why?
- What's your favorite movie and why?
- What is something that really gets on your nerves and why?
- If you could go anywhere in the world, where would it be and what would you do there?
- Who is someone you really admire and why?

You can add your own questions to the list—just make sure they require more than a yes-or-no answer.

Listener: What's something that really gets on your nerves and why?

Speaker: I hate when people cut in line. First of all, I think it's totally inconsiderate and unfair. Secondly, it makes me feel like the person couldn't care less that I'm even there.

Listener: So, it really bugs you when people butt in line. It's not fair, and you feel like you're being ignored. Sounds like it makes you really mad.

Speaker: It does!

Listener: Who's someone you really admire and why?

Speaker: My dad, because he works really hard and even though he's tired when he gets home, he always asks me about my day.

Listener: I heard you say you really respect your dad because he's a hard worker and he has time for you no matter how tired he is. Sounds like you really love him.

When you're the speaker, be careful to keep your answers short and simple. Otherwise the listener will have trouble remembering what you said.

When it's your turn to listen, if an answer is longer than you can remember, ask the speaker to repeat the part you forgot. Then try reflecting back what you heard.

Each time you play this game, you'll become more skilled at reflective listening. You'll become more experienced doing the kind of listening that's important for anyone who's interested in getting along better, understanding other people, and resolving conflicts.

Using Reflective Listening When There's a Conflict: Two Examples

Farah got into a conflict situation with her friend Kim at the mall. Farah spotted a group of kids she knew from her youth group and she wanted Kim to go with her to talk to them. That's when the conflict started:

"Let's Go Hang Out"

Farah: Come on, Kim. Let's go hang out with the kids from my youth group for a while.

Kim: No way. I don't know any of them and I'll feel like a real idiot just standing there with nothing to say. Plus I want to go check out the jeans that are on sale.

Farah: Come on Kim, just for a few minutes.

Kim: *(irritated)* I said no. I don't want to hang out with them.

Farah: Last time we came to the mall, we talked to some kids from your soccer team and I didn't complain.

Kim: Look, stop pressuring me. I don't want to go!

Farah: *(stops, takes a few deep breaths, realizes there's an escalating conflict, and decides to tune in to how Kim feels with reflective listening)* So you're feeling like I'm pressuring you right now.

Kim: Yes! You *are* pressuring me and I don't like it.

Farah: You're ticked off at me, aren't you?

Kim: Yeah, I am. I really don't want to be with those kids. I don't know any of them and I'm gonna feel totally out of it just standing there while everyone talks to you.

Farah: *(kindly)* So you're afraid you're going to feel left out.

Kim: *(a little calmer now)* Right.

Farah: I know how you feel. When it's a big group like that, I feel kind of shy, too.

Kim: Really? You always seem so sure of yourself.

Farah: I don't always *feel* that way. Listen, maybe you can start looking for jeans and I can go talk for just a few minutes. You don't have to come with me if you really don't want to.

Kim: *(smiling)* Okay.

Reread the scene between Farah and Kim. Can you pick out the place where the conflict started to turn around?

You're right if you said the conflict changed when Farah took a deep breath and tried to understand how Kim felt. You're also right if you said when Farah did some reflective listening instead of just trying to convince Kim to do what she wanted her to do.

Now take a look at a conflict between Tony and Dimitri. Dimitri thinks Tony looks at him funny whenever they pass in the hall. Today he goes up to Tony and confronts him:

"Who Are You Looking At?"

Dimitri: Who are you looking at?

Tony: Why are you asking me that?

Dimitri: 'Cause every time I see you, you give me some kind of look.

Tony: What are you talking about?

Dimitri: You give me looks and I don't like it.

Tony: You're crazy!

Dimitri: Oh, yeah? I'll show you how crazy I am!

Tony: *(takes a deep breath, calms himself, tries to understand where Dimitri is coming from)* So you feel like I'm dissing you with my looks, is that right?

Dimitri: You are, and I want you to cut it out!

Tony: *(respectfully)* Listen, I didn't mean to make you uncomfortable.

Dimitri: No?

Tony: No. I've been looking at you, not because I don't like you or anything like that. The truth is, I wanna do what you did to your hair, and I've been trying to get a good look at it.

Dimitri: *(points to the streaks he's recently put in)* This?

Tony: Yeah. I guess I should have just asked you.

Dimitri: You should have.

Tony: I didn't mean to have it turn into a big deal.

What moved this conflict in the direction of a solution rather than a big fight? Tony decided to take a step back, breathe, and figure out what Dimitri was thinking and feeling. He used reflective listening to make sure he understood and to show that he wanted to resolve the problem. Try doing the same thing yourself next time someone is mad at you and see what happens.

Good Listening Builds Good Relationships

Practice good listening as often as you can. If you start doing this on a regular basis, you'll notice that many of the people you normally get into conflicts with will begin to act differently with you. For most conflicts, you can help the situation enormously if you make the effort to really listen—to pay close attention, encourage the other person to explain, and use reflective listening to make sure you understand. Over time, you will find yourself getting along better with the people in your life and having fewer conflicts.

Use Win/Win Guidelines

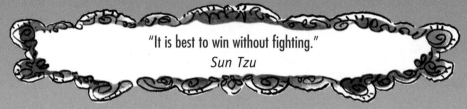

"It is best to win without fighting."
Sun Tzu

In this chapter you'll discover:

- **six powerful guidelines for resolving conflicts**
- **ways to practice the guidelines**
- **how to use the guidelines in real-life conflicts**
- **answers to some of your tough questions about being a conflict solver**

You've been reading about being willing to work out problems and listen to what the other person has to say. Now you're going to find out how to put it all together so the next time you're faced with a conflict, you'll have a system that really works—one where everybody feels better in the end. That's what happened for 14-year-old Frank:

"My sister and I used to fight a lot. I started to see that it just wasn't worth it. You never feel good when you fight against someone else. Even when you win you lose. Now when we have problems we usually talk it out. We understand what bothers each other and we try not to do those things as much. It feels a lot less stressful to be getting along. We're both a lot calmer."

Frank and his sister found a way to deal with conflicts so they both ended up feeling better—a win/win situation. To make this happen in your own life, you can use a system called Win/Win Guidelines. These guidelines will give you a fair way of working out conflicts with people at home, friends, classmates, teachers, teammates, and practically anyone else you can think of.

There are six Win/Win Guidelines. While you're learning them, do all of them in order. But once you know how to use these guidelines, you'll be able to skip some, depending on the situation.

The Win/Win Guidelines

1. Cool off.
2. Talk the problem over using I-messages.
3. Listen while the other person speaks, and say back what you heard.
4. Take responsibility for your part in the conflict.
5. Brainstorm solutions and choose one that's fair to both of you.
6. Affirm, forgive, thank, or apologize to each other.

To make sure the Win/Win Guidelines work, it's important to agree to these basic rules:

Rules for Using the Win/Win Guidelines

- Tell the truth.
- Be respectful.
- Attack the problem, not the person.
- No blaming, no name-calling, and no negative face or body language.
- Work together toward a fair solution.

To start using the Win/Win Guidelines at home, show this chapter to your parent or guardian. Ask for a family meeting to introduce the guidelines to everyone. If you all agree to give this a try, it will be easier to work out the conflicts you have. You might even want to make a poster showing the Win/Win Guidelines and the rules for using them. Put the poster on the refrigerator, on a wall in the kitchen, or someplace else where everyone can easily see it.

In school, if you're not already doing some kind of conflict resolution program, share this book with a teacher, guidance counselor, or principal and ask one of them to introduce the Win/Win Guidelines to your class or even to the whole school. There are lots of schools where everyone is committed to working out conflicts peacefully. Kids in these schools feel safer and more relaxed, and even learn better. That's because they don't have to deal with the constant stress of conflict.

Now let's take a look at how the Win/Win Guidelines work. First you're going to read a description of each guideline. After that, you'll see an example of what it's like to resolve a conflict using all six guidelines together.

1. Cool off.

If your heart's pounding a mile a minute and you're ready to jump out of your skin, it's impossible to think straight, let alone find the right words to solve a problem. That's why it's super-important to cool off first. Sometimes this means walking away for a while and doing something to calm yourself down. You might get a drink of water, take some deep breaths, wash your face, or do a few laps around the block. After you're calmer, you can go back and talk things out.

If you're not sure how to cool off, you'll find lots of ideas in the next chapter. See pages 68–83.

Don't skip this step. Here's why: It's next to impossible to work out a conflict in the heat of anger. This is true for you and for the other person, too. If you're trying to resolve a conflict and it's not working, one or both of you may need time to cool off.

2. Talk the problem over using I-messages.

Ever notice how when someone gets mad, what comes out of the person's mouth usually starts with the word *you*? "*You* did this." "*You* said that." "*You're* an idiot!" These statements are called "you-messages" because they use the word *you* to blame and accuse the other person. Starting with you-messages almost always makes the problem worse. The other person usually throws a you-message right back, like "*You* started it!" or "*You're* the one who's an idiot!" And then the fight escalates.

Real words from the survey

"I first take three deep breaths and give the person an I-message about how I feel."

When you start with *I*, it can be a lot different. People are less likely to feel angry or defensive when they hear words like "I'm annoyed at what you said" or "I feel bad when you talk to me that way." Starting with *I*, and avoiding sarcasm or blame, allows you to say what's on your mind without adding to the conflict.

What Are I-Messages?

I-messages are statements that start with the word *I*. The most important thing about them is that they don't accuse or blame. Because of this, the other person is more likely to listen to what you have to say. Most I-messages tell three things:

- how you feel

- why you feel that way

- what you want or need

Here's an example: Suppose you and your brother are playing a game together on the computer and he's hogging the mouse. You think, "You jerk! Give me that mouse!" But you know that'll just start a fight. So you say this instead:

I feel bad, 'cause I've been waiting so long. I want a turn, too.

There are other ways you could get this I-message across. You could start by saying what you want or what you see happening. Here are two different approaches you might take:

I want a turn, too. I've been waiting patiently and it's not fair for you to keep the mouse so long.

OR...

I've been waiting a long time to play. It's not fair if we both don't get a turn.

Sometimes I-messages can be simpler:

As long as you keep the focus on what *you* need—and avoid letting blame creep into your voice—I-messages will generally lead to better results than you-messages. Also, be aware of your body language. If you deliver an I-message with crossed arms or clenched fists, you're going to send out angry vibes, even if your words are respectful.

As you can see, using an I-message doesn't mean giving in when something isn't right. In fact, it's just the opposite: I-messages are direct and honest. They let you speak your mind in a way that's respectful. It takes courage to speak the truth and to make an effort to figure out how to do so without being mean. But flexing that courage muscle is worth it, because I-messages open doors to problem solving. You-messages close them. Look at these two scenes to see the difference:

Hey—I was just gonna sit down here.

No way. I got here first.

Wait, this isn't worth fighting over. Let's just pull up another chair and we can both sit here.

Try It

Read these situations where people use you-messages. Come up with respectful I-messages that Brian, Rachel, Lisa, and Gary could use instead:

- Brian and Shawna are playing basketball. Shawna pokes Brian in the eye by accident. Brian says, "You dork! Watch what you're doing!"

- Rachel and Lars are working on a project. Lars forgot to bring in his notes and materials. Rachel says, "You're so irresponsible! Can't you ever remember anything?!"

- Sulin told Lisa she couldn't go to the movie because she had to study. Later, Lisa heard that Sulin went to the movie with someone else. Lisa says to Sulin, "You're such a liar!"

- In gym, Gary had trouble climbing the rope to the ceiling, and Paulo made fun of him. Gary says to Paulo, "So what if you did climb better? You're nothing but a stupid jock!"

What If an I-Message Doesn't Work?

I-messages usually help ease conflict situations. But what if that doesn't happen? One student told me, "I tried using an I-message, but the other person told me to shut up." If something like this happens to you, ask yourself these questions:

Did the other person need more time to cool down? Sometimes when people are really angry, they don't think—they just snap back with a mean response. When this happens, it's best to give them a little space. You

Think About It

Who is someone you recently had a conflict with? Did you talk to the person using you-messages? What I-message could you have used instead?

might say something like, "I can tell you're really mad. Let's talk about this later." Then walk away calmly. After cooling off, the person might be more willing to work things out.

Does the person tend to bully other people? If so, using I-messages might not work. Kids who bully usually don't care about getting along—they get satisfaction from making you feel bad. How you handle a situation like this depends on lots of things, like who else is around, whether you feel that you're in danger, and other issues. If it feels safe, you might try telling the person to cut it out and then walk away with your head held high. Step 7: Be Smart About Bullying (pages 99–117) gives you lots more information and ideas for dealing with this kind of problem.

Do you think that saying shut up is the way this person generally handles conflicts? In that case, don't give up on I-messages. If you keep trying to talk things out respectfully, after a while the other person might follow your lead. Learning to resolve conflicts peacefully is a skill that takes time and practice. Don't give up if it doesn't work right away. If you're persistent, patient, and respectful, you may solve the problem over time. Plus, you'll have shown someone else a new and better way to deal with conflicts.

3. Listen while the other person speaks, and say back what you heard.

For a refresher on reflective listening and other listening skills, take another look at Step 3, pages 36–49.

When you're trying to resolve a conflict, listening skills are a powerful ally. Try to put aside your own thoughts for a minute and focus on what the other person is saying. Give your full attention. Use reflective listening, where you say back what you've heard. This will show that you're really listening and trying to see the other person's point of view (even if you don't agree). If you do this, the other person may be willing to do the same for you. Once you've heard the person out, you'll both be feeling calmer and better able to find a solution, as in these examples:

"I Thought It Was Mine"

Kevin: Whoa! I worked hard on that book report, and you just wrote all over it!

Mark: *(embarrassed)* So you think I did this on purpose?

Kevin: Duh. Yeah. How can I turn it in like that?

Mark: I thought it was mine. I can explain to Ms. Sayed if you want me to.

"I Meant to Ask"

Rhea: I've asked you not to borrow my clothes without asking! You wore my sweater last night and now it smells like french fries!

Lindsay: Oops. I can see you're really mad at me for doing that. I meant to ask, but you weren't home.

Rhea: Then you should have worn your own clothes!

Lindsay: You're right—I shouldn't have worn it without asking. Do you want me to wash it?

Rhea: Yes. And please ask next time.

Lindsay: I will.

Mark and Lindsay used reflective listening to understand where the other person was coming from. Doing this stopped their conflicts from getting out of hand. Getting in the habit of reflective listening will also help you become a better all-around listener, someone who can really tune in to another person's point of view. The majority of all conflicts are based on misunderstandings. Reflective listening will help you hear each other out and understand each other better.

4. Take responsibility for your part in the conflict.

Most people find it a lot easier to blame someone else than to admit being wrong. This is a common part of conflicts. Some people are afraid to tell the truth about a mistake or wrong action because they believe that if they do, they'll look bad or get in trouble. And sometimes, people blame others strictly out of habit.

This is a challenge for nearly all of us. We know that blaming keeps the conflict going, but that doesn't make it easier to admit when we've done something that caused a problem. When we find the courage to take responsibility for what we've done that's harmful or hurtful, we can start solving the problem. And when we're brave enough to go first, the other person will be more likely to admit his or her part.

These two scenes illustrate what I'm talking about. In the first one, neither person takes responsibility:

"What You Said": Scene 1

Will: I'm really mad about what you said about my mother in front of the other kids at the bus stop.

Joe: I didn't say anything. That must have been Craig.

Will: No, it was you. I heard it with my own ears.

Joe: You must be dreaming. I never said anything about your mother. You're makin' it up.

Will: You're a liar and I can prove it.

Joe: You're the liar. *You* were bad-mouthing my sister in the lunchroom yesterday, and then you pretended you didn't know what I was talking about when I brought it up!

Will: You're nuts! Get off my case.

Joe: Make me!

Now watch how differently things turn out when one person quits blaming and owns up to what he's done:

"What You Said": Scene 2

Will: I'm really mad about what you said about my mother in front of the other kids at the bus stop.

Joe: What did I say?

Will: You said she was fat and ugly.

Joe: *(takes a deep breath)* Okay, I admit it. I did it because of what you said about my sister yesterday.

Will: What?

Joe: You said she's stupid, and stuff like that. She can't help it if she's bad at reading. That was mean.

Will: Well, what you said about my mom was mean, too!

Joe: Listen, I didn't mean that about your mom.

Will: Really?

Joe: I know it was mean.

Will: Okay, I didn't mean what I said either. I was just trying to get even.

You respect yourself more when you're honest, and so do other people. Sometimes when you take responsibility for hurting someone, you need to go further and do something to make things better. That's called making amends, and it's exactly what Tanika decided to do:

> ## Think About It
> Think of a conflict you had recently where things didn't work out well between you and the other person.
> - How were you responsible for starting the conflict or keeping it going?
> - How was the other person responsible?
> - What could you have done to work things out?

"I Was Wrong"

Tanika: Shari, I need to talk to you. I was wrong for sending around that email about you.

Shari: So it *was* you. I knew it! The harm's been done. I have nothing to say to you.

Tanika: Listen, I really want to apologize. I shouldn't have done it. When I went home and thought it over, I realized how mean it was. I felt terrible.

Shari: How could you say all those nasty things about me and then send it out to five kids? You really want to ruin my life, don't you?

Tanika: No, I really don't, and I'll email all those kids back and tell them I was wrong.

Shari: How can I trust you after what you said about me?

Tanika: Because I'm going to make it better.

Shari: Why did you do it in the first place?

Tanika: Because I thought you were trying to take Lynn away from me. We've been best friends since second grade, and now she's always hanging out with you.

Shari: So that's why! But that's no reason to try to ruin my life!

Tanika: I'm really sorry.

Shari: You should be. Anyway, I like Lynn, but I always liked you, too. I thought we were friends. That's what hurt the most.

Tanika: I wish I never sent that email. Will you please accept my apology?

Shari: As long as you never do anything like that again. Are you really going to email everyone back and tell them you didn't mean it?

Tanika: Promise. Come on, I'll write it up right now. You can watch.

Try It

Think of a conflict where you blamed someone instead of taking responsibility. What ended up happening? Now consider going back to the person, telling the truth, and doing something to make things better. You may be less nervous if you first rehearse what you'll say.

Admitting to doing something wrong takes a lot of courage. Even though this was hard for Tanika, she managed to summon up the strength to do the right thing. She knew it would be worse for herself and her friends if she didn't take responsibility. And when she thought of the harm she had done to Shari, she realized she would have been just as angry if someone had done the same thing to her. Now the friendship can mend and Tanika can feel proud of herself for not backing down to fear.

5. Brainstorm solutions and choose one that's fair to both of you.

There are lots of solutions to every problem. Too often we think there's only one, or maybe none. But it's just the opposite! Your brain is capable of coming up with tons of great ideas if you are open. Next time you are involved in a conflict, ask your brain if it can give you at least three different ways of solving it. And listen to the other person's ideas, too. Between the two of you, you should be able to come up with something that works—a fair compromise. If you're willing to compromise, no one

Great solution!

has to actually lose in a conflict. You each may need to give in a little bit, but you'll both end up winning because you've worked out the problem instead of fighting. Here's an example. Joanie and Steph are best friends. They've been having an ongoing conflict over the issue of smoking. Today it came to a head:

"I've Made Up My Mind"

Joanie: I've made up my mind—I'm gonna try smoking. Kyra's bringing cigarettes to the party tonight.

Steph: Joanie, you couldn't mean that! You can't start smoking. What about track?

Joanie: I'm just gonna try it. Trying isn't starting.

Steph: But smoking's addictive. Kyra's sister was going to just try it, and now she smokes a lot.

Joanie: Lots of kids smoke, and they're fine.

Steph: Not runners like us. Smoking's gonna ruin it.

Joanie: What, if I smoke you won't be my friend?

Steph: Of course I'm your friend—you're my best friend!

Joanie: Then don't try to tell me what to do. It's *my* life! *(turns away in anger)* You're really getting on my nerves.

Steph: *(stops and takes a breath, realizes she needs to take a calm approach)* Wait, Joanie. *(lowers her voice)* Look, you're my best friend and I care about you, that's all.

Joanie: Then quit bugging me. Smoking looks cool, and I really wanna try it.

Steph: Listen, my uncle started smoking when he was 14, and now he has to breathe through a hole in his throat with a tube sticking out. It's totally gross.

Joanie: That's not gonna happen to me.

Steph: And I'm afraid you *will* get hooked, and then it'll come between us, because smoking totally bothers me. Do you really want to do it just to be cool?

Joanie: Well, it *does* look cool . . . *(hesitates)* I know it's not good for my breathing in running. But I just said I'd try it.

Steph: Is there some way we can compromise on this?

Joanie: Compromise? How?

Steph: Like I'll stop talking about it if you'll just give the whole thing a little more thought.

Joanie: But I promised Kyra I'd do it tonight. She'll be ticked off if I go back on what I said.

Steph: So you feel like Kyra's gonna get mad if you don't do it?

Joanie: Yeah, I think she will.

Steph: Is there some way you can get out of it?

Joanie: *(thinks for a minute)* Maybe I can tell her I'm coming down with a cough and I don't want to make it worse.

Steph: Or maybe you can just say you decided to hold off.

Joanie: No, she'll be mad. But I could say I want to see how she likes it before I try it.

Steph: Yeah, but if she likes it, what then?

Joanie: I'm gonna have to make that decision.

Steph: Maybe you could just skip the party. Make an excuse like your dad said you can't go. You told me he said you could say that if you ever needed to.

Joanie: Kyra'll just want me to go anyway and tell him I'm somewhere else.

Steph: Is that the kind of person you're gonna let influence you?

Joanie: *(considers Steph's words)* Let me think about this . . .

Steph: You mean it?

Joanie: Yeah, I do. You can be a pain, but I know you care. And you do have a point. Kyra's popular and everything, but she's not so honest. And she's pushing pretty hard when it should really be up to me.

Talk About It

Think about a conflict you've read about or seen in a movie or on TV. With some friends, brainstorm as many solutions to the conflict as you can. See how many ideas you can come up with.

Steph took the lead here and was able to convince Joanie to work with her in finding a win/win solution to a big conflict. When you start letting your brain work in this direction, you'll be amazed to discover how many solutions there can be for practically any conflict. By being respectful, hearing the other person out, and looking together for ideas to solve the problem, you can bring lots of possibilities to light.

6. Affirm, forgive, thank, or apologize to each other.

Once you've worked out your conflict, it's a good idea to say something nice to the other person. This shows you're sincere and that you really have worked out the problem. Here are a few things you can say:

- "I'm glad we're still friends."

- "I like having you for a brother."

- "I know I get mad sometimes, Gran, but I really love you."

- "I forgive you for what you did and I accept your apology."

- "Thank you for hearing my side."

- "Thanks for being willing to come up with a solution."

- "I'm sorry I accused you of doing that."

- "I apologize for hurting your feelings."

- "I wish I hadn't talked behind your back."

You can also shake hands or hug, depending on the situation. Even giving a smile after you've worked out a conflict shows the other person that you're not mad anymore.

Putting It All Together

Now it's time to see what it's like to solve a conflict using all six of the Win/Win Guidelines. The kids at Leo's school have been using them all year. Two days ago, his friend Kent called him a stupid wimp because he wouldn't join Kent and some other kids in writing cruel words on Jimmy Bowman's locker. Leo said it was wrong to treat someone that way and he wanted no part of it. When Kent called him a wimp, Leo pushed him against the wall. Kent pushed back and the other kids had to pull them apart. Leo and Kent haven't talked since. Up till now they were pretty good friends.

Leo feels really bad about his fight with Kent. He knows that Mr. Johnson, the guidance counselor, lets kids use a space next to his office as a place to talk through conflicts. This morning, Leo asked Mr. J. if they could do this. Mr. J. told him, "If you can get Kent to come by, the talking area will be free at three o'clock. I'll be right next door in my office if you need help working out the problem."

Leo got Kent to agree to meet with him. Here's how their talk went:

"Ready to Talk"

Leo: *(takes a deep breath, speaks to Kent)* We've had two days to cool off. I'm ready to talk. How about you?

Kent: *(breathes deeply)* I'm cool.

> 1. Cool off.

Leo: Listen, I don't want to let the other day ruin our friendship. But I was really mad when you called me that name.

Kent: *(breathes deeply, stays calm)* You were mad 'cause I called you a wimp.

> 2. Talk the problem over using I-messages.

Leo: Yeah—really mad. The reason I backed off from writing on the locker wasn't because I was scared. It was because I felt sorry for the kid you were doin' that stuff to.

Kent: *(respectfully)* You really felt bad for him.

Leo: I did. He's not the coolest kid around, but that's no reason to make his life miserable.

Kent: I just wanted to have some fun. All the guys were really into it.

Leo: So you were just going along with the other kids.

Kent: Yeah. It was just a joke.

Leo: What if the joke was on you?

Kent: But it wasn't . . . and I didn't appreciate being pushed.

> 3. Listen while the other person speaks, and say back what you heard.

Leo: I was really angry. *(both boys take a breath and look at each other)* Okay, I'll say it first, I shouldn't have pushed you. But you shouldn't have called me a stupid wimp.

Kent: I was just foolin' around; I didn't mean it. Sorry.

Leo: I'm sorry too. *(pauses for a moment)* I guess we should think about a solution now.

> 4. Take responsibility for your part in the conflict.

Kent: We said we're sorry. What else do you wanna do?

Leo: Let's think about what we can do if this kind of thing happens again. *(pauses)* I have to be honest—I feel bad when the guys wanna do mean things like that.

> 5. Brainstorm solutions and choose one that's fair to both of you.

Kent: Hey, it's just for fun.

Leo: To you maybe. I saw what it did to my brother when he used to get picked on in eighth grade. I don't wanna make anyone feel that bad.

Kent: But Jimmy Bowman *is* a loser.

Leo: That's what they used to call my brother, but I know better. And Jimmy Bowman— he's a human being.

Kent: So what am I supposed to do next time the guys wanna tease him? If I say no, they'll probably start in on *me*.

Leo: If we stick together, maybe it won't be so easy for the guys to single one of us out.

Kent: *(thinks for a minute)* Power in numbers?

Leo: Yeah.

Kent: Okay.

Leo: Thanks for being willing to talk. I feel a lot better now.

Kent: Me, too. I didn't like being mad at each other.

> **6.** Affirm, forgive, thank, or apologize to each other.

This conversation wasn't easy for Leo and Kent, but they cared about their friendship and were willing to try to work things out. They knew and used skills for talking and listening to each other in a respectful way. They followed a plan—the Win/Win Guidelines—to keep themselves on track. Following the guidelines helped them solve their problem, stay friends, and make a decision they both felt good about.

"Yes, But" Questions

"Yes, but wouldn't I be better off just walking away and forgetting about the problem? I'm afraid if I try to talk about it I might make it worse."
Sometimes it *is* appropriate just to walk away and forget about the problem. The question to ask yourself is, can you do this? What happens sometimes is that we walk away and stew. We keep thinking about the problem and what we should have said. We talk about it with everyone *but* the person involved. Then the problem gets

Think About It

Who can help you if you're having trouble resolving a conflict at school? At home? Where can you find a helpful, trusted friend or adult in other situations? Think about places you can turn for help with your most challenging conflicts.

worse or we end up thinking and worrying about it all the time. If that happens to you, it's a clear signal you need to talk to the person you had the problem with. If you have trouble doing this, ask a teacher, a counselor, another adult, or a peer mediator to help. Sometimes dealing with a problem directly feels scary, especially if you haven't done it before. But each time you do, it'll get a little easier. Plus, talking things over will help you release the bad feelings you would otherwise be carrying around inside.

"Yes, but this girl lies. My guidance counselor mediated a conflict we had, and the girl promised to stop calling me names, but when no adults are around she still does it. I told the counselor and the counselor said something to her, but she acted like I was making it up. What am I supposed to do?" Ask the guidance counselor to sit down with the two of you again. In this setting, talk to the girl about what's been happening. Use I-messages to tell her how you feel. If she continues to deny what she's doing, don't argue—just keep restating your original point. Here's an example of how you could do this:

"I Thought We Agreed"

You: After we came here before, I thought the name-calling would stop. But it didn't. I feel really disappointed that you didn't keep your promise.

Girl: *(to counselor)* Uh-uh. She's making it up. I'm not doing anything.

You: *(looking directly at girl and restating your point without arguing)* I felt really bad when you called me those names at lunch.

Girl: I don't know what you're talking about.

You: When I walked by you and your friends yesterday, you called me the b-word and they all started looking at me.

Girl: *(to counselor)* No way. She's just trying to get me in trouble.

You: *(looking directly at girl, restating your point respectfully)* I thought we agreed that the name-calling wasn't going to happen anymore.

By bringing the problem out in the open and confronting the girl in the presence of your counselor, you give a clear message that you are unwilling to allow it to continue. Stating your feelings and the problem without arguing allows you to come from a place of strength and maturity. If you argue back, you and the girl will just get into a war or words, and then the problem will never get solved. Standing up for yourself in a respectful way is your best route.

"Yes, but I've tried to get my teacher to help when there's a conflict, and he always says, 'You'll have to handle it yourself.' What should I do?" First of all, ask yourself if you've tried to work out the problem on your own. It's always best to try this first before going to a teacher, except if you're being bullied. In that case, you'll need support right away. If you've sincerely tried to handle a conflict and nothing's worked, talk to a trusted adult at school or at home. Ask the adult to set up a meeting with your teacher and the principal so you can get help solving the problem.

Be a Role Model

One of the students I interviewed for this book said, "Kids need to learn peacemaking so when they grow up they can teach their own kids to be peaceful and help other people. Sometimes kids can help each other be kind."

By using conflict resolution, you will not only change the way you relate to others, you'll serve as a role model. You might not realize it in the moment, but other kids and adults will be taking notice. The courage you show in trying to work out conflicts respectfully may give other people the courage to do the same.

> **Real words from the survey**
>
> "If we stopped fighting, our lives would be much better."

Manage Your Anger and Gain Control

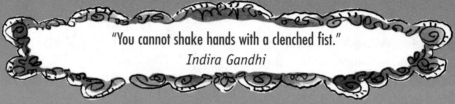

"You cannot shake hands with a clenched fist."
Indira Gandhi

In this chapter you'll discover:

- **what your anger pitfalls are**
- **how your body reacts to anger**
- **ways you can calm down, keep your cool, and help yourself manage anger**
- **what to do when you're faced with an angry person**
- **how to stop anger from leading you to a physical fight**

When I go into classrooms and talk with kids, one thing is always true: everyone struggles with angry feelings. Anger is part of being human. You don't have to feel guilty if you get angry sometimes. The problem with anger is not the emotion itself, but the way people handle it. Learning how to deal with anger is super-important if you're serious about being a conflict solver. That's what this chapter is all about.

What Are Your Anger Pitfalls?

Everybody handles anger a little differently. There may be times when you cope with it pretty well. Most of us, though, tend to fall into some negative habits that make the angry feelings (and the conflicts that go with them) worse instead of better. Think of these as your anger pitfalls. To find out what yours are, see which questions you answer yes to:

Real words from the survey

"I get mad when people get an attitude and put you down."

"I get really angry when I'm playing basketball and I miss a shot and my sister says, 'Ha-ha, you missed!'"

"Here's what gets me mad, when you get blamed for something you didn't do."

When I'm angry with someone, this OFTEN happens:

✓ I lose my ability to think straight.

✓ I say or do something I regret later.

✓ I push, hit, punch, or kick.

✓ I curse or yell.

✓ I call the person names, give a nasty look, or use some other kind of put-down.

✓ I walk away and gossip about the other person.

✓ I say and do nothing right then, but afterward get even.

✓ I sulk or feel crummy inside.

✓ I stuff my feelings down and try to ignore them.

✓ I take it out on someone else.

✓ I decide the other person is an idiot.

Practically everyone has one anger pitfall or another. To overcome yours, you first need to know what they are. Then you can start to change them.

Why Do So Many People Have Trouble Managing Anger?

Anger is a difficult emotion, and most people have trouble handling it. One reason has to do with the body's built-in system for surviving. When someone says or does something to get you mad, you automatically feel one or more physical sensations in your body: Your heart might start to pound. You might feel shaky or tense. Your stomach might go into a knot. You might start breathing harder or feel your face heat up. You might feel a jolt of energy, like an electrical charge shooting up the center of your body. This charged energy can make you feel more alert, but it doesn't help you think more clearly. In fact, people's ability to think can actually shut down when they become charged with anger. Instead of thinking through what we want to do, we react, often by either striking out or pulling back. This physical reaction is known as the *fight-or-flight mechanism.* Some people

automatically strike out with words or fists—they *fight*. Others may feel numb or paralyzed, like they don't know what to do. Or they might feel like running away or hiding. That's *flight*.

The fight-or-flight mechanism is built into our brains and bodies. You see, years ago when our ancestors were cave people, there were times they needed to either fight or *flee*—take flight—in order to survive. Back then the dangers humans faced were often life threatening, so people had to react quickly. The problem is, we all still have the fight-or-flight mechanism working inside us. It leads many of us to handle being threatened the way cave people did thousands of years ago. Your personal fight-or-flight mechanism will probably kick in, for example, if the person sitting next to you in the lunchroom sticks out a foot to trip you so you drop your tray and spill everything. You might go into an angry "fight" reaction and haul off and clobber the person. Or, if you lean more toward "flight," you might run off screaming and yelling or hide your head in embarrassment. In either case, the conflict won't get resolved.

But if you know how to recognize when you're going into fight-or-flight mode, you can turn it into *choice* instead. You have several very positive choices you can make to handle anger, simple but powerful techniques that are yours to learn and use. So read on!

Three Secrets to Getting a Handle on Anger

The key to managing anger is to learn how to *choose* your response instead of just reacting. When you do this, you take control of yourself rather than let the anger carry you away. Choosing a response gives you power; reacting takes your power away. To keep yourself from reacting without thinking, you can use the secrets of "Stop, Breathe, Chill."

1. Stop

When someone's actions make you mad and you feel yourself starting to react, give yourself a message to stop. That's right, stop—just for a moment. Just long enough to regain control.

When you stop, say the word in your head and picture a big red stop sign. Feel what you feel, but don't act on it. Exercise your power of choice. By doing this even for a split second, you prevent yourself from reacting in ways you might regret later. That's the first secret to regaining control of yourself. But just stopping isn't enough.

2. Breathe

Taking a few deep breaths can help you calm a racing heart. The most powerful kind of breathing you can do when you get mad is called abdominal breathing. When you're in a conflict, five abdominal breaths can actually lower your heart rate and restore your sense of control. Many of us are used to a quicker, more shallow kind of breathing, so you may need to practice abdominal breathing before it will come naturally. Here's how you can learn it:

Sit up tall and put your hands on your abdomen (the lower part of your stomach). Imagine this part of your stomach being a balloon that you can fill with air. Inhale (breathe in) slowly and deeply through your nose, and imagine the air going right down into that balloon. Gently expand your lower abdomen (the balloon part) and your lungs at the same time.

Hold the breath deep inside for a moment. Imagine the air circulating to every part of your body, relaxing you.

Gently exhale (breathe out) through your nose. As you exhale, slowly deflate the balloon by pushing the air out with your abdominal muscles.

Try It

Practice abdominal breathing. As you breathe, focus on the movement of the breath in and out, and on the calming effect it has on your mind and body. Try repeating this five times. Feel your pulse and thoughts begin to slow down.

The next time you're in a conflict and feel the anger rising, say "stop" to your immediate reactions, and use deep breathing to calm your brain and body.

3. Chill

Picture yourself in a conflict. Imagine stopping and breathing so you don't react in ways you'll regret. To help yourself chill out even more, there are a number of things you can do. You've already read about calming statements that you say silently to yourself. These can be a *huge* help. Here's why: Negative thoughts can fuel anger big time. Thoughts like "I hate that kid" or "I'm ready to blow my top!" make you even madder. Sure, angry thoughts are going to pop into your head when someone disses you or confronts you. But if you keep focusing on them, you're going to end up making yourself feel worse. This is where calming statements come in. They'll help you put yourself back in control of *you*. At that point, you'll be better able to handle what the other person's doing.

A great thing about calming statements is that you don't necessarily have to believe them in order for them to work. That may sound strange, but each time you feed your mind a calming statement, your brain will start to take over and help you calm down (even if the rest of you doesn't think it's possible). Trust your brain to do its job. There's an even better payoff: The more you use calming statements, the more you'll start to believe they're true. It's like reprogramming your brain.

My favorite calming statement is "I can handle this." It's simple, empowering, and makes me feel like I really *can* cope. Here are other calming statements you might want to try:

- "I can keep my cool."

- "I am in control."

- "No one can make me feel bad about me."

- "I have the power to stay calm."

Write About It

On a sheet of paper, write down at least ten things that help you chill out. Keep your list in your notebook. Make a copy to put up in your room, too. Or make your list into a colorful poster that makes you feel good when you look at it. Next time you're mad, use one of your personal chill-out ideas to help yourself calm down.

Think About It

1. Choose one of the calming statements on this page or make up one of your own. It should be short and positive. Be sure to state it in terms of *now:* "I am calm" rather than "I will be calm."

2. Write down your calming statement and hang it up in a place where you'll see it every day.

3. Read it, say it, repeat it, and picture it coming true as often as you can. After a while you'll start feeling your calming statement come to life, even when you're in the middle of a conflict.

- "Peace is inside me now."
- "I have the strength to stay out of fights."

If you're in a conflict and your calming statement isn't helping, or if you need more time to think about what to say and do, walking away for a few minutes or longer is another way to chill. Before you walk away, say something like, "Look, I'm too mad to talk right now. I'll talk with you later." Then be sure to come back and work out the problem when you've calmed down. Or maybe the other person needs more time. If so, use words such as, "I know you're really mad now. I hope we can talk later." Then give it another try when the person seems calmer.

Once you've walked away, here are some other helpful ways to chill out:

- Go to a quiet spot.
- Put cold water on your face.
- Listen to music.
- Look at the sky and focus on its color.
- Think of something funny.
- Get some exercise.
- Read, draw, or model clay.
- Clean out a drawer.
- Work on a project that interests you.
- Play with a pet.
- Squeeze a rubber ball or a crumpled wad of paper.
- Take a bath or shower if you're home.

- Remind yourself that you're bigger than he problem.
- Put it in perspective—know this moment of anger will pass. Feelings always shift and change.

So, there you have it—three secrets for getting a handle on anger: "Stop, Breathe, Chill." Try using this strategy next time you're in a conflict. If you stick with it, I promise you, "Stop, Breathe, Chill" *will* put you in greater control.

Decide Not to Get Hooked

When someone says or does something to get you really mad, imagine the words or actions as a glob of slime being thrown in your direction. You have three choices: You can catch the slime and hold onto it, you can fling it back at the person, or you can let it drop on the floor and walk away from it. By making a conscious decision *not* to get hooked by someone else's negative words, you maintain your power rather than give it away. As one teen said, "I refuse to let *their* words run *my* day."

Some people walk around all day with other people's put-downs taking up space in their brains. Or they walk around with thoughts of getting even. If you do this, you're hurting yourself more than you might realize. Negative thoughts can drain your energy and even affect your health if you hold onto them for too long. They can make you feel madder and madder and prevent you from thinking of ways to cope with the anger. But you don't have to stay hooked like that. Try doing one (or all) of these things to release angry thoughts and feelings:

Write down what you're mad about. This is just for you. Let all the bad feelings flow out onto the paper, even the ones you're embarrassed to admit. When you've let them all out, tear the paper up and throw it away. Afterward you're likely to feel better, because once the feelings are out on paper, they're out of your brain.

Give yourself a set amount of time to stew. If possible, allow yourself about thirty minutes. Do something to release the angry energy while you stew. If you're home, you might go for a run, lift some weights, or do a few jumping jacks. If you're at school, wash your face and get a drink, or do some deep breathing. While you're doing these things, allow the anger to move through you and out. Then, when your set time is up, tell the feelings, "I'm finished with you—goodbye." Or tell yourself, "Okay, that's enough fuming. I'm letting it go now."

After that, you'll need to use some self-discipline so you don't allow your mind to keep going back to the thing that's making you mad. Get busy with a project or some kind of physical exercise. Another great way to refocus is by helping someone else. Offer to help a friend who's having trouble with an assignment, or pitch in to help fix a meal at home. This way, you transform the angry energy into something positive. You'll feel good and the other person will, too.

Talk to a trusted person. Make this confidential. The worst thing you can do is start gossiping about the person you're mad at, because that will only escalate the conflict. When you talk about what's bothering you, do it with the intention of getting the bad feelings out of your system rather than getting even. Explain to the person you speak to that you're talking about this so you can get it off your chest and go forward without the burden of bad feelings.

Move on. Moving on might mean letting go of what happened. It also might mean coming up with a plan of action. For example, you might decide to talk directly to the person yourself to try to resolve your conflict. Or you might want to write the person a note asking if the two of you can sit down together and work out the problem. Or maybe you'll decide to ask your teacher, a counselor, another adult, or a peer mediator to help the two of you solve the problem.

Unhooking from a habit of anger is worth it. My son Tim learned this at an early age. As a kid, he let his bad temper take over and spent way too much time feeling angry and annoyed. He remembers that starting to change when he consciously decided to unhook from his own anger reactions. These are Tim's words, "I started to realize that there was nothing to be gained by giving in to my temper. But by not letting it get the best of me, I was in control. That made me feel good." Tim is now a police officer who uses anger management and conflict-solving skills in all areas of his life, including his work. He told me, "I'm really glad I learned to do this when I was a kid."

If You Feel Like You Can't Control Your Anger

Sometimes anger can well up so strong and so often that we feel like it's out of our control. If this is the case with you, it's critical that you talk to a trusted adult. By talking to someone now, you'll be able to start breaking the pattern of angry outbursts so you can feel better about yourself and your life. You don't have to do this alone. There's someone in your life (probably more than one person) who cares enough to help. Find that person now. You can also call the toll-free National Youth Crisis Hotline number to talk to someone confidentially: 1-800-448-4663.

Make Yourself Zinger-Proof

Sometimes our anger is triggered by other people's zingers—sarcastic comments and put-downs. On TV shows and in movies people use zingers all the time, and when we see and hear them, we usually laugh. Zingers can seem clever and cool. But when they're flying at us, it can be a different story. If the zingers are directed at you, you might feel annoyed, angry, or even outraged. Sure, there may be times when you can just laugh them off, but if someone insults you with a zinger, you have a right to feel mad. And so does the person who might be on the receiving end of your zinger.

The Survey Says

How mean do you think kids generally are to each other?

- 11% said kids are not mean at all or are a little bit mean.
- 89% said kids are somewhat or very mean to each other.
- What do you think?

You might feel like mean put-downs are a part of life that can't be avoided. Some of the kids who took the survey felt this way. One boy wrote, "There will always be kids who enjoy teasing, tormenting, and just being mean to other kids." Another said, "I don't think it's possible to change another person's meanness." And a girl wrote, "There isn't a lot you can do because lots of people stereotype each other and like to talk mean about others." Maybe you can't stop every person who takes pleasure in throwing out zingers or saying nasty things, but there are still things you can do to address the problem. The first and most important thing is to decide not to join in. That's the choice a middle schooler named Abby made for herself:

"The kids in my class are constantly using zingers. Every minute, someone's trying to outdo the next person with sarcastic remarks or put-downs. I refuse to get involved. It's not my thing and I don't need to build my self-esteem by making someone else feel bad. So I either walk away or think about something else."

Write About It

Create your own personal insurance policy against letting zingers affect you. Make three lists:

- all the things you're good at, even little things

- all the people in your life who care about you, adults as well as kids

- happy memories from as far back as you can remember to the present

These lists are your insurance policy. When someone says something that gets you down, don't let it take up space in your brain. Instead, focus on something from one of these lists. Put your energy toward the stuff that makes you feel better, not worse.

The Survey Says

Top 5 Things Kids Suggest for Stopping Meanness

1. Talk honestly.

2. Get to know and understand each other.

3. Work together on projects.

4. Show how it feels to be teased.

5. Have adults help.

What Do YOU Say?

What are some things you think can help kids stop being mean to each other?

Abby has the right idea. Why have your day ruined or ruin someone else's day with put-downs? Sure, it's hard to pull back from a zinger match, or to let harsh words bounce off you. But, like Abby, you actually have the power—and you can find the courage—to make this happen.

Some kids feel like they can't survive without giving a zinger back each time they hear one. Maybe you're one of these people. It's normal to want to protect yourself. But the truth is, you'll survive better if you let the put-downs fly right past you. That's what Abby does. NOT throwing out zingers at others helps her keep feeling good about herself, and other people are less likely to send zingers at her.

If the zingers are directed at you and you feel yourself reacting inside, remember the "Stop, Breathe, Chill" strategy. Focus on a calming statement that also reminds you of your own strength: "I won't give anyone else the power to make me feel less than I am." Then leave the scene.

If you don't want to just walk away, you can say something like: "I respect myself too much to listen to this." Rehearse your statement in front of the mirror. Practice standing tall and strong and looking at the person directly as you say the words. You'll want to come across as matter-of-fact, not angry or defensive. Then practice walking away with your head held high. The next time a moment comes when you want to walk away from a zinger, you'll be able to look and sound cool and in control, even if you don't feel that way inside. Over time, you will find more confidence. And other kids will learn not to mess with you because they won't get the result they're looking for. The more you react, the more it encourages them. You have the power to break that cycle.

What if you're someone who throws zingers at other people? Don't give yourself a hard time for what you've done in the past. Kids try to survive any way they can. Having a bad habit doesn't mean you're a bad person. Now's your opportunity to make a different choice for the future. Ask yourself these questions:

1. Why do I feel like I need to put people down?

2. Is it worth the damage I might be doing to others?

3. Is there some other way I can make myself feel good without using zingers?

Make a plan for what you can do the next time zingers are flying so you don't have to use them, too. If you had a good friend who wanted to stop using zingers all the time, what would you advise him or her to do? Consider trying this advice yourself.

Talk About It

Do you have a friend who's as tired of put-downs as you are? Talk together about ways you can help each other stay zinger-proof. Agree on a plan of action for getting away from put-downs. You might use a signal like putting your hands in your pockets. Or maybe you can agree to say something like, "This is probably making _____ uncomfortable." Or, you can walk away together.

Protect Yourself from Other People's Angry Vibes

Part of managing conflict is figuring out how to deal with other people's anger. What do you do if someone's just plain mean and directs that anger at you?

Here's a technique from an exceptional guidance counselor named Virginia Abu Bakr. Her strategy can help you calm yourself when you feel angry, and it can help you stop the fear that often comes when we're faced with someone else's anger or meanness. Try it yourself:

Peace Shield

Close your eyes and think of something that makes you feel happy and peaceful. Let the good feelings fill you up. Now picture an invisible shield of protection gathering around you, keeping the good feelings in. Choose a color for your peace shield. Imagine it keeping you calm and protecting you from all harm. Take a slow deep breath to "lock in" the power of your peace shield. Keep your eyes closed and focus on this image.

At the start of each day, close your eyes and put your peace shield in place by picturing it just the way you locked it in before. Remind yourself that you will have the shield with you all day, wherever you go. Use it any time you face mean or angry words and actions from kids or adults. Picture your peace shield *completely* protecting you, locking in your safety and locking out all harm.

What works so well with this technique is that when you feel protected by your shield you'll be less likely to feed into the other person's anger. For example, when someone's shouting at you, if you breathe deep and surround yourself with your peace shield, you won't be as tempted to shout back. That way the other person's anger will be less likely to escalate.

Light Shield

You can feel even more powerful and protected from other people's negativity by picturing a second shield, a light shield. Start by imagining yourself safe behind your peace shield. Then think of someone who has a lot of anger or meanness. See yourself completely protected from this person's negativity by your peace shield. Now picture yourself sending out a beam of light to surround the angry person. Imagine the person contained behind a shield of light created by your beam.

After getting used to the ideas of a peace shield and a light shield, try using them both. Try them when you feel anger rising up inside of you and want to regain control. Also try them when you're confronted by someone who is angry or using cruel or nasty words. Visualizing the shields will give you a greater sense of control. It will also keep your mind focused on something calming rather than allow it to be taken over by anger or fear. Then, if you need to talk to the person, talk. If you need to leave, leave. Either way, keep your peace shield in place the whole time. Keep the light shield in place as long as the other person remains angry or threatening.

When Anger Leads to Physical Fighting

Sometimes people try to stay calm when there's a conflict, but their anger is ignited when the other person hits, shoves, or just won't stop saying mean things. Many of the kids I surveyed and interviewed talked about this. Here's what Ty told me:

"I was hanging out with my friends and these kids started calling us names. At first I tried to ignore them, but then it got worse. I told the kid who started it to shut up. He wouldn't, so I pushed him. When he pushed me back I got so mad I knocked him off the fence he was sitting on. He cut his arm and he was bleeding. I felt good that I hurt him. But later when I got home and thought about him lying on the ground with a bloody arm, I started to feel guilty. If I had to do it again, I would've walked away."

When someone gets you really mad, you might want to lash out. And in the moment, it can feel good, just like it did for Ty. But afterward, you may end up

Real words from the survey

"I remain calm until they hit me, but then I start hitting them back."

"Sometimes people make me so mad that I punch them."

"I think fighting helps get your anger out."

"Why do people fight? Why are they so angry?"

feeling bad. Another consideration is that when your anger leads you to fight, you can do serious physical harm. The person you're fighting might hurt you, too. And someone could have a weapon. Way too many cases already exist where angry acts between kids turn into violence that harms or even kills.

Ty was on the right track when he talked about walking away. If you're angry enough to shove or punch, leaving the scene is probably the smartest thing you can do, too. Sure, you might miss that charge you get from fighting, but you'll also miss the consequences—like detention, punishment at home, a bad reputation, guilt, and physical harm.

Some people believe they need to save face if someone says or does something to get them mad, and fighting is the only way to do it. Many kids, mostly boys, wrote about this in the survey. But fighting is a dead end. The more you rely on fighting to save face, the more violent your life will become. It's so important to find the strength *not* to let anger draw you into physical aggression. Having the courage to resist fighting shows that you don't have to prove your strength through violence.

You have many tools to use instead of your fists. Regain control with "Stop, Breathe, Chill." Then, if the other person isn't threatening you physically, use one of these alternatives:

Try talking respectfully. If the person is shouting, lower your own voice instead of raising it. Shouting escalates anger. Try to understand the other person's point of view. Use the listening and speaking skills you read about and practiced in Steps 3 and 4.

Suggest a time-out. If the person is a friend or family member, say something like, "This really isn't worth fighting over." Suggest that you take a time-out and talk about the problem when you're both calmer. Again, try to keep your voice steady and low. Take deep breaths to help yourself do this.

Put yourself in the person's place. If you feel you can reason with the person, try *empathizing*. Empathy is a sincere understanding of how another person feels. To empathize, you need to imagine how you would feel if you were the other person. You might say, "I know you're really mad at me now, and I can see why." Hearing this may ease the other person's anger. If the person becomes calm enough, suggest talking about the problem together. You may want the help of an adult or a peer mediator.

Think About It

Close your eyes and take five slow, deep breaths. Picture yourself feeling relaxed, confident, and in control of your life. Now imagine someone saying or doing something that might normally ignite your anger so you'd want to fight. Think about all the ideas you've learned for calming down and responding to the other person. Write down three ideas you can do instead of responding with an angry fight. Remember your choices and use one of them the next time you're in a tense, angry situation with someone else.

Play it safe. Don't let someone else's anger put you at risk. If you believe the other person is going to start fighting physically, don't keep trying to talk it over. Leave the scene as calmly and quickly as you can.

If you're worried about your future safety, tell an adult what's going on. This isn't tattling. Asking for help is a necessary thing to do if someone has hurt you or is threatening to do so. By not talking to an adult, you practically guarantee that the person will hurt you at some point.

Take Control

You have the power to handle your own anger. You also have the power to be a conflict solver in the face of other people's anger. The strategies you've learned in this chapter can put you in control. Make the strategies yours. Remember, too, that you really *can* make a difference for others. Your effort means there is one more person in the world—YOU—who knows how to make it a less violent place through strong, courageous choices. Think about what the world would be like if more and more kids learned to do this. Spread the word.

Real words from the survey

"If we talk it out, there's a good chance that no one will be hurt."

STEP 6

Learn to Manage Stress and Stay Calm, Cool, and Confident

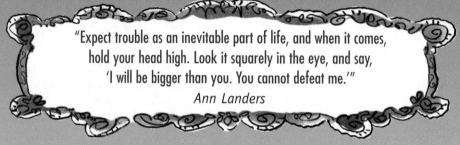

"Expect trouble as an inevitable part of life, and when it comes, hold your head high. Look it squarely in the eye, and say, 'I will be bigger than you. You cannot defeat me.'"
Ann Landers

In this chapter you'll discover:

- **what stress is and why it happens**
- **how to know when you're feeling stressed**
- **sure-fire ways to stay cool and in control in stressful situations**
- **strategies for building your self-confidence so stress won't get the better of you**
- **ways to feel calmer all the time**

STRESS. Even the word can make us feel edgy. When we talk about stress we usually mean stuff that upsets us and causes a reaction in our bodies and minds. But there's actually good stress, too. Like the stress you feel before an exam that makes you study harder. Or the stress you feel before a big game that helps you be more alert and focused. Still, too often the stress we experience is the negative kind—like when you have a ton of homework, plus baseball practice, and then you find out that the report you thought was due next week is really due tomorrow.

So what does stress have to do with conflict? Plenty. When you're stressed, you feel tense, anxious, on edge, jittery, wound up, or trapped. At times like these, you're more likely to get into conflicts and *less* likely to handle them well. By now you know that being a conflict solver and a peacemaker requires a clear head and a LOT of self-control. But when stress overtakes you, you're not fully in control. That's why a whole chapter in this book is devoted to helping you get a handle on stress. The more you practice the techniques in this chapter, the calmer and cooler you'll be when you're involved in a conflict.

What exactly *is* stress? It's that tension you feel inside your body and your brain when you react to something that's uncomfortable or threatening. Sometimes you can feel stressed when you try something new or difficult. Stress can even come from your thoughts. Demands and pressure cause stress, too. The pressures kids and teens deal with are enormous. Maybe you've put pressure on yourself to live up to an image of what you think you should be. Or maybe you get pressure from your friends to do things you know you shouldn't be doing. Or perhaps family adults put pressure on you to do well in school, make certain teams, or dress a certain way.

The middle school kids I interviewed mentioned all of those pressures and others, like these:

- juggling lots of homework and activities

- making and keeping friends

- getting or staying thin

- being pressured to act cool, smoke, drink, have sex, do drugs, or go to parties

- problems with friends

- problems at home

- not feeling good about yourself

- bullying

- being left out

- body changes and questions about sexuality

- things outside of school and family, like terrorism, war, and pollution

Sometimes people deal with stress by drinking, using drugs, smoking, overeating, or not eating enough. Doing these things might seem to help temporarily, but in the end they add even more stress, not less. In this chapter you'll learn some very positive ways to handle stress and make yourself stronger rather than weaker.

Think About It

• What stresses you out? In your notebook, write down the worries and pressures that give you the most stress.

• Is there something you already do to handle your stress? If so, what? Does it help? Make things worse? How? Is it a healthy choice?

You're not alone if you're feeling stress—people of all ages experience it on a daily basis. That's the downside. But there's an important upside, too: You have the power to get a handle on how stress affects you. Stress comes from inside of you. That may sound strange, but it's a fact. Outside pressures can lead to stress, but your reaction to these pressures comes from the inner you. Because of this, you actually have the ability to manage stress. Sure, there will always be stress in life, but once you've learned how to deal with your reaction to it in positive ways, you'll have the ability to look stressful situations in the eye and not be defeated by them. Ask any successful person: It's not about avoiding stress, it's about handling it. When you can do this, you'll be able to triumph over the problems you face.

Anger is a big source of stress, and stress can contribute to feelings of anger. So if you haven't already checked out Step 5 (pages 68–83), be sure you do. Many of the suggestions there for dealing with anger can help you when it comes to stress, too.

Do You Know Your Stress Signals?

Certain situations can trigger stress in each of us. Here's what kids who talked with me or took part in the conflict survey said about how stress affects them:

"When I'm stressed out my brain feels like two cymbals hitting together."

"When my grandpa yells at me before I come to school I feel totally stressed. Then I want to take it out on my friends."

"I feel stress in my hands. They do things I don't want them to do."

"When people are coming at me with questions, asking me this and that, my head starts to hurt."

We'd love to hear from you!

Help us make Free Spirit books the best they can be—let us know your thoughts, reactions, things you found helpful, things that weren't so helpful, and any other comments you'd like to give us about this book. Use the space below (or send us a letter, an email, or a photo if you'd prefer) to tell us how you put *The Kids' Guide to Working Out Conflicts* to use—the more details the better! Thanks for your feedback!

Comments:

your name (please print) _____

street _____

city/state/zip _____

email _____

❏ *I give Free Spirit Publishing permission to use my comments*
   in ads, brochures, mail, catalogs, and any other promotions.

Signed: _____ Date:_____

www.freespirit.com • help4kids@freespirit.com • 800.735.7323

Want to know more about making positive choices, coping with challenges, keeping it together, and making a difference?

Free Spirit can help! We're the award-winning source of SELF-HELP FOR KIDS® and SELF-HELP FOR TEENS®. We know the issues young people face, and we have the information and tips you need to succeed. Mail this card for a FREE catalog. (And have one sent to a friend!)

Send me a Free Spirit catalog! (I am a ❏ kid ❏ teacher ❏ parent ❏ other)

name (please print)_____

street_____

city/state/zip _____

email _____

and send one to: (He/She is a ❏ kid ❏ teacher ❏ parent ❏ other)

name (please print)_____

street_____

city/state/zip _____

email _____

Visit www.freespirit.com to download excerpts, quizzes, and more! free spirit PUBLiSHiNG®

Free Spirit Publishing
Your SELF-HELP FOR KIDS®
and SELF-HELP FOR TEENS®
source for over 20 years.

BUSINESS REPLY MAIL

FIRST-CLASS MAIL   PERMIT NO. 26589   MINNEAPOLIS MN

POSTAGE WILL BE PAID BY ADDRESSEE

free spirit PUBLiSHiNG®
Department 842
217 Fifth Avenue North, Suite 200
Minneapolis, MN 55401-9776

Free Spirit Publishing
Your SELF-HELP FOR KIDS®
and SELF-HELP FOR TEENS®
source for over 20 years.

**NO POSTAGE
NECESSARY IF
MAILED IN THE
UNITED STATES**

BUSINESS REPLY MAIL

FIRST-CLASS MAIL   PERMIT NO. 26589   MINNEAPOLIS MN

POSTAGE WILL BE PAID BY ADDRESSEE

free spirit PUBLiSHiNG®
Department 842
217 Fifth Avenue North, Suite 200
Minneapolis, MN 55401-9776

As these comments show, we all react to stress in our own unique ways. Our reactions are signals to us that we're under stress and need to do something to relieve it. Use this quick self-test to check out your own stress signals:

When I'm under stress . . .

✓ Everything gets on my nerves.

✓ I feel anxious, worried, or jumpy.

✓ My thinking gets foggy.

✓ I start to get dizzy.

✓ My heart pounds.

✓ My head aches.

✓ I can't sleep even though I'm tired.

✓ I want to sleep all the time.

✓ My stomach hurts.

✓ My palms get sweaty.

✓ I feel angry all the time.

✓ I have a short temper.

✓ There are bad thoughts in my head that won't go away.

✓ My skin breaks out.

Which stress signals apply to you? Are there others you experience that aren't on the list? Get to know your own personal cues that stress is overtaking you. By paying attention to your stress signals, you'll know when it's time to do something to relieve them in a positive way.

Just growing, changing, and trying to survive whatever grade you're in can put you under stress. Added demands and pressures can pile more stress on you until your body and mind start to say "Enough!" If that's happening to you, it's a sign that your body and mind are trying to keep you in balance. So, if your body starts saying, "I need some downtime," listen to it. Giving yourself the

Think About It

What relaxes you? Close your eyes and think about it right now. How many relaxing things can you come up with? Write down at least five things that help you feel cool and calm. Make yourself a promise to do one of them for at least fifteen minutes each day.

break you need when you need it will help keep you healthy. You'll refresh yourself so you can tackle the things you have to do.

By the way, lots of us turn to TV, video games, or the computer when we want some downtime. If this is true for you, consider this: Violent or aggressive games and programs actually raise your stress level, not lower it. In fact, studies have revealed that viewing violence on the screen makes people more aggressive. Do yourself a favor. Cut back on your screen time and find other ways to de-stress. You'll be better off for it in the long run.

What's on Your Mind?
Find the Calm Confidence Within You

Did you know that daydreaming is actually good for you? (As long as you don't do it in the middle of math class!) There's a kind of focused daydreaming called *visualization* that can help you feel calmer from the inside out. When you visualize, you use your imagination to picture something in full detail.

Try it now. Picture the sun on a bright summer day. Now picture it shining down on a sandy beach with rolling waves. Picture yourself jumping into the water. Feel the water on your skin and smell the salty breeze.

There. You've just visualized, and for that moment you may have felt like you really were at the beach and nothing else existed. Your mind was focused only on that pleasing image. That's how visualization works. It helps you direct the focus of your mind to images that make you feel at ease, confident, and in control. Your mind is a very powerful tool, but most people don't know the secrets to harnessing its power.

A top benefit of calming yourself through visualization is that it can lower your level of tension and anger when you're in a conflict or any other stressful situation. Ever notice how when you feel calm you don't react as much to what other people say and do? This is true for all of us. When we're tense, every little thing can get the best of us. When we're relaxed, something negative might happen, and we'll feel like it's no big deal.

Here are two visualizations to help you get calm and confident:

Picture a Peaceful Place

Sit or lie down in a comfortable spot. Take five slow, deep abdominal breaths. Imagine your mind is a blank movie screen. Project the color blue onto your screen. Picture it as a soothing shade of blue like the sky on a clear spring day. Allow this image to fill your mind completely. Now project onto your blue screen an image of a place you've been where you felt happy, relaxed, peaceful, and safe. It could be as close as your own home or someplace far away. It could also be a place back in time, like your grandmother's kitchen when you were five. Let this peaceful place completely fill the screen of your mind. Allow it to grow so big that the screen you've projected it onto melts away.

> Wondering what abdominal breathing is? Pages 71–72 explain how to do this deep form of breathing.

In your mind's eye, step into your peaceful place. Walk around and notice the sights, sounds, and colors. Breathe deeply and inhale the scent of your peaceful place. Allow its calmness to fill your chest, head, arms, and legs. Allow the good feelings you had when you were last there to fill your heart and spread out into every cell, the way sunlight touches everything around it. If any distracting thoughts come into your mind, put them on a cloud and let them float away. Then gently bring your focus back to your peaceful place, letting its peace wash over you inside and out.

Once you've tried this a few times you can expand the vision of your peaceful place to make it even more wonderful. You might add a special pet or anything else that would make you relaxed and happy. This peaceful vision is one you can return to whenever you

Record It

Tape record yourself reading the "Peaceful Place" visualization above in a calm, slow voice. Play it back whenever you need to de-stress. Before long you'll have the whole thing memorized.

feel stressed, frightened, angry, sad, or anxious. Going back to your peaceful place will enable you to bring good feelings inside yourself no matter what's going on around you.

See the Confident You

Close your eyes and take a few deep breaths. Go to your peaceful place and allow it to completely relax you. Now picture yourself stepping into your peaceful place looking strong, sure of yourself, and content. Imagine being exactly as you'd like to be. Picture every detail. Notice your smile, the brightness of your eyes, the way you walk, the way people respond to you.

If you can imagine yourself calm and confident, you can make it happen. Your brain will grasp onto all the positive images you're sending its way and help you make them real. The image of yourself at peace and feeling confident will give you the strength to deal with whatever comes your way.

One small caution here: If you picture your confident self but your mind starts arguing with you, saying, "No, this isn't possible," firmly ask your mind to be quiet. Return your focus to the confident you. *You* are stronger than the chattering voice of your mind. You don't need to buy into negative thoughts.

Use Empowerment Statements

Visualization is one way to "train your brain" to support you from a place of calm strength. Another way is to help yourself focus on all you are capable of by using empowerment statements. An empowerment statement is something you say to yourself that helps you see and strengthen your abilities and personal power. Empowerment statements help you replace negative thoughts and feelings about yourself with thoughts that make you feel stronger and more confident. This is another incredibly important tool to help you deal with whatever challenges life puts in your path.

Here are some examples of empowerment statements:

"I am strong, capable, and filled with self-respect."

"The voice of strength, fairness, and compassion lives inside me. I can use it now."

"I am worthy of respect and happiness."

"I have the ability to overcome any difficulty that stands in my way."

"I use my power for peaceful purposes."

"I am happy, confident, and in charge of myself."

"I am able to stay calm and cool."

Empowerment statements help you replace negative thoughts that wear you down with thoughts that connect you to powerful parts of yourself that may have been hiding. The strong, sure parts of you are in there! Using empowerment statements helps you bring them out. Choose one (or more) empowerment statements to say to yourself every night and every morning. That way you will start and end each day helping yourself believe the *best* about you.

Write About It

In your notebook, write down as many of your positive qualities as you can think of—things that show you how strong and capable you are and can be. Also write some qualities you want to develop. But don't stop there. Ask your family, your close friends, and other people who care about you to tell you what positive qualities they see in you. Save your list. Add to it whenever a new quality comes to mind. Read it over whenever you need to remind yourself of the capable, confident person you really are and the ways you are continuing to grow your personal power.

Activate the Secret of 5/25

As I've studied, practiced, and taught conflict resolution and peacemaking over the years, I've learned that it takes about 25 days in a row to break an old habit or create a new one. If you want to develop the habit of staying cool, calm, and in control in the presence of stress or anger, you'll definitely want to learn the secret of 5/25. Here it is:

By practicing a new skill or technique

for a total of 5 minutes a day

for 25 days . . .

. . . you'll turn something new and unfamiliar into a life-changing habit. This really works.

Visualization and empowerment statements get easier with practice. When you first start doing them, your mind might be filled with all kinds of distracting thoughts. Use the secret of 5/25 to train your mind to sit still and notice what *you* want it to. It's like training a frisky puppy. Each time you guide your mind to the place you want it to go, it will "listen" more and more instead of jumping all over the place.

So train your mind to be cool, calm, and confident! Practice these three things every day for a combined total of 5 minutes:

- Go to your peaceful place.

- Visualize the confident you.

- Strengthen yourself by repeating at least one empowerment statement several times.

Continue for 25 days or nights in a row to make this practice a habit. With the habit in place, your feelings about yourself will become more positive and hopeful. Continuing to use the techniques will build your calm strength and internal power. The practice of 5/25 will ensure that they become a solid part of your life.

More Ways to Stay Calm and Cool

When you keep yourself calm and grounded, the stresses of everyday life become a lot easier to handle and you'll be less likely to get into a conflict. Here are more ways to manage stress and keep yourself in balance. Use them to stay cool, confident, and in control no matter what's going on around you.

Get some physical exercise! Ever notice how great you feel after you've participated in a gymnastics meet, a lively game of catch, or something else that gives you a real workout? There's a reason you feel good: *endorphins.* Endorphins are substances in your brain that are released when you do vigorous exercise. You've probably heard of a runner's high. That's endorphins at work. It's sad that people take drugs to get the same feeling endorphins can give them for free and without harm to their minds and bodies.

So choose a physical activity you like, and do it as often as you can—three times a week at least. And when you feel the stress of life building up, stop, breathe, and then chill out with physical exercise. You have the power to determine the way you feel. Use it.

Express yourself. Are you someone who likes to write? If so, get yourself a journal. Did you know that many people who journal regularly are mentally and physically healthier? Journaling helps you get your feelings out and make sense of life. Creating art or music can accomplish the same thing. One boy I talked to said that every time he played his saxophone he felt transported to a different space, one where he always felt happy and complete. You don't have to be especially talented to reap the benefits. Just by doing something that lets you express yourself, you'll feel better. And be sure not to judge what you create. Write, draw, paint, sing, model clay, or play the drums for the sheer pleasure of it.

Do things that make you feel sure of yourself. When do you feel strong, happy, and confident? When you spend time outdoors? Kick back with a great book? Take part in sports or arts activities? Hang out with friends? Perhaps you have a hobby like cooking or collecting stamps. Or maybe you like helping other people or doing a job like baby-sitting or lawn-mowing. When an activity is

Think About It

Think of everything in life that gives you joy. Make a list of these things. Now make sure to do something from your list each week, even each day if you can.

healthy and helps you feel good about yourself, it's right for you! Do it as often as you can.

Be thankful. It's easy to focus on the negative, and that's what lots of people do. But by focusing on what you're grateful for, you can improve your mood and outlook. Plus, you'll feel calmer in the face of stress. What are you thankful for in your life? Make a list, and count even the smallest things. Can you think of 5 things? 20? 50? 100? Once you get started, you may be surprised. Be a detective on the lookout for every detail of life you might feel grateful about. Is there someone you can say thanks to? Say it! Review your list often and keep adding to it.

Build bonds of closeness. Did you know that having loving people to be close to is one of the keys to mental and physical health? It's important that some of these people be adults, too. A dad, a stepmom, a foster parent, an aunt, a cousin, a grandparent, an adult friend—any or all of these people might be able to spend time with you and offer a listening ear.

If you don't have any adults who are available to spend time with you, seek out a *mentor*. Think of the adults you know who you trust and respect at school, in your community, or at your place of worship. If you could use a supportive adult in your life, don't wait for someone else to make it happen. Try approaching someone you trust. Explain that you admire and respect the person and could use someone to talk to. See if the person would be willing to make some time for you at least once a week. You can talk, hang out, or do things you both enjoy. Having an adult friend in your life can spell the difference between loneliness and feeling connected. Know that you never have to struggle by yourself. Someone out there cares.

Fact

A study compared kids who have close relationships with parents, teachers, and friends and kids who don't. The study found that it was much less common for kids with close relationships to:

• be victims of violence

• act violently toward others

Find Out About It

If you need help finding a mentor, ask a counselor, teacher, or youth leader for advice. Here's an organization that can match you with a caring adult in a one-to-one mentoring relationship. Your parent or guardian can sign you up and your local agency will pair you with an adult in your community. To find the local agency contact:

Big Brothers Big Sisters Association • 230 North 13th Street • Philadelphia, PA 19107 • (215) 567-7000 • www.bbbsa.org

Friendship with other kids is important as well. Some people have lots of friends, some have one or two. You're in a good spot if you have even one good friend close to your own age, someone you trust and care about and who cares about you. If you're not sure what to do to create new friendships, try taking an interest in the person you want to get to know. Ask questions and listen more than you speak. Ask if you can join in, and be willing to compromise when you do activities. Asking to join in can be hard, but the more you do it, the easier it gets. If people say no, don't push the issue. Find someone who will say yes. A great place to find people to hang out with is through clubs and after-school activities. Some schools have friendship groups where kids can get to know other kids. See if there's one in your school, or ask the principal or counselor about starting one.

De-Stress with Yoga and Meditation

These days yoga and meditation have become the craze. Celebrities talk about the benefits, and ads are filled with people in yoga or meditation poses. Though it may seem like a fad, the simple truth is that yoga and meditation can unquestionably de-stress and improve your life if you do them on a regular basis.

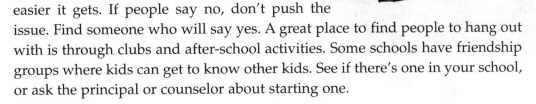

"When I practice yoga, I feel whole. I feel nothing is beyond my reach."
Diane, age 13

Learn Yoga

Yoga is an age-old practice of balancing the mind and body through breath, movement, and mental focus. Yoga began in ancient India and is now used in many parts of the world. With yoga, you move through a series of poses called *asanas.* As you do, you breathe steadily and deeply and focus your mind to help your body hold the poses. The practice of yoga helps you to calm and sharpen your mind, strengthen your body, and gain inner power. Yogis (people who practice yoga regularly) understand that the strength and power gained through yoga is intended to be used for peaceful purposes only. In fact, some yogis begin each yoga session by picturing peace in themselves and in the world.

If you'd like to give yoga a try, you're in luck. Most communities now have yoga centers, and some schools are starting to include yoga instruction as part of physical education. If your school isn't one of them, talk to your physical education teacher about offering yoga in gym class. Or see if a teacher will help you contact a local health club or yoga center about starting an after-school club or giving lessons where kids can learn and practice yoga. One of the teachers in your school might already practice yoga. Maybe he or she would be willing to set up a lunchtime or after-school class.

Meditate to Relax Your Mind

Meditation is a way of clearing your mind of its usual thoughts and helping it go to a more relaxed place. By meditating regularly, you can help yourself become a calmer, more focused person all the time; you'll teach your mind how to settle down and stay cool. Here's one way to do it:

1. Find a quiet spot to sit, either in a chair or on the floor. If you're comfortable, sit on the floor cross-legged, on a pillow. (You'll be able to sit longer if your seat is higher than your knees, so position the pillow accordingly.) You might want to lean against the wall for support.

2. Set an *intention*—by saying or thinking to yourself something you really hope to accomplish: "I intend to feel good about myself." "I intend to get along better with my family." "I intend to help my school be a more peaceful place."

Once you've done this, let go of your intention and trust that it is possible for it to become real. Letting go means that you don't have to keep concentrating on what you intend in order for it to happen in your life. Setting an intention doesn't guarantee that it will come true for sure. But it's a way of guiding your mind to remember what you want to create.

3. Begin to breathe slowly and deeply through your nose. Close your eyes and focus on the rhythm of your breath. Feel the air going in and out through your nose, and keep focusing only on that. When thoughts start to pop into your head, gently let go of them and bring your focus back to the rhythm of your breath. Imagine putting each thought on a cloud and letting the cloud float it away, just as you did when you envisioned your peaceful place.

4. Focus on a calming image.

Your peaceful place is one. A favorite of mine is the ocean. I picture the movement of the water as though I'm on a transparent raft where I can see the water below. I imagine the gentle rocking feeling of floating on the water, and the feel of the sea air on my body. If you try this, focus on the feeling of your breath going in and out through your nostrils and on the image of the ocean around you.

Some people use a word or sound as their focus. You can choose a word that makes you feel relaxed, like *love, peace, hope, calm, confidence,* or *joy.* As you breathe in and out, try to fit the sound of the word with the rhythm of your breath. Or use two words. On the inhale, think "Calm," and on the exhale, think "Confidence."

5. Keep breathing and focusing. When you first start meditating, continue this for five to ten minutes in one sitting. You can build up to longer periods if you like. Meditating several times a week for fifteen minutes will make a big difference in your life. Doing it daily will bring you the greatest benefits of all.

If you find yourself thinking a lot when you're trying to meditate, don't get frustrated. This happens to everyone. Your mind is used to going wherever it

Fact

A study at the Medical College of Georgia showed that meditation actually lowered high blood pressure in teenagers. Teens who participated in the study also reported that meditation:

• increased their ability to concentrate at school

• decreased school absenteeism and behavior problems

• helped them handle relationships better

• led to sounder sleep and increased energy

• eased headaches

• reduced stress

Can you imagine getting all these benefits from the simple practice of meditation?

wants to go. Each time your mind drifts away, ease it back to the focus you have chosen. Each time you bring your mind back to this calm place, it will become more comfortable letting go of all the thoughts, worries, and fears that tend to clog it up and keep you stressed. Eventually when you meditate, you'll be able to go to a place of calmness that's similar to the semi-dreamy state you experience right before you fall asleep. (My yoga teacher told me that she started meditating when she was in her early teens. She'd meditate every day before going to school, and sometimes she'd get into such a relaxed place she'd almost miss the bus! If you're worried about this happening to you, set a timer.)

To start meditating and make it part of your life, set up a special space where you can do this at home. It might be in your room or somewhere else where you can be quiet and alone. Create an area that suits your taste and personality. You might set up a chair or cushion facing a window. Cover a small table or box with a handkerchief or scarf you like. Place objects that have special meaning to you on your table—pictures of people you care about, rocks or shells you've picked up and saved, or other things that help you feel calm and happy. Then set your chair or cushion in front of the table and meditate.

Choose Calmness

Remember, the calmer you are, the fewer conflicts you're going to have and the less you're going to go around feeling angry. Wouldn't it be great to be calm enough inside that you didn't feel affected by the stuff that normally upsets you? Now you know strategies for making that happen. Make the decision to manage the stress in your life. By calming yourself, you'll also breathe a little more peace into our world.

Be Smart About Bullying

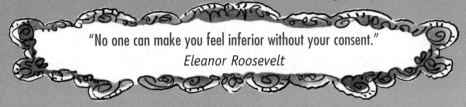

"No one can make you feel inferior without your consent."
Eleanor Roosevelt

In this chapter you'll discover:

- the difference between teasing and bullying
- how to stop teasing that goes too far
- why people bully
- how to stop bullying if you're doing it to others or if someone is doing it to you
- answers to your important questions about bullying

Bullying and conflict can go hand in hand. When someone tries to bully you, you might react by saying or doing something that makes the situation worse. Next thing you know, the person's going after you at every opportunity, maybe even getting friends to pitch in.

Or maybe there's someone at your school who you get into arguments with all the time. At some point that person might go a step further and start partnering up with buddies to put you down whenever you walk down the hall. Then what started off as a conflict turns into bullying. The downward spiral of violence—either emotional or physical—continues with each new incident.

Thirteen-year-old Eli told his story about the emotional toll bullying can take:

"It started when I was in sixth grade. We had just moved, and I was the new kid in the class. The first day of school, everyone seemed to know each other but me. No one talked to me, and I ended up eating lunch alone.

"It went downhill from there. Kids started calling me names. Sometimes they would look at me and laugh or make jokes. There was only one kid in my class who would talk to me. Sometimes he would sit with me in the lunchroom, but after a while the other kids started picking on him for doing it, so he stopped.

"I don't know what I did to make them treat me so bad. They called me a weirdo. Maybe I was different and maybe my clothes weren't as cool as theirs, but so what? I was always decent to people. That didn't seem to matter.

"I started getting stomachaches. I begged my dad to let me stay home from school. He just thought I was having trouble adjusting. He had no idea what was going on, and I didn't want to tell him. I was afraid he'd talk to my teacher, and then things would get even worse.

"Finally one night Dad asked me if something was wrong. I started to cry and the whole story came out. He ended up talking to the guidance counselor, and even though I didn't want him to, it turned out to be the best thing. The counselor talked to me the next day. She told me that the way the kids were treating me wasn't my fault. Part of me didn't believe her, but another part was relieved. She went into our class and started doing lessons on bullying. I think she talked to my teacher, too, because after that Mr. Khan always made sure I had someone to eat with, and if he saw anyone acting mean to me he would say something.

"This year I'm in seventh grade and I have some good friends. The kids have stopped picking on me, but there's this other kid they make fun of now. I want to stick up for him, but I'm scared I'll get picked on again if I do. I really feel bad about not helping him, because I know how miserable he must be."

Eli's story is a sad one, though it's encouraging that things got better for him. The saddest part was that Eli felt too scared to stick up for the other kid who was being picked on. Unfortunately, many kids make the same decision. Fear stops them. This creates an even bigger problem, because each time we look the other way, we allow the mean behavior, and the hurt, to continue. This chapter will help you deal with teasing, put-downs, and bullying in all situations—if you're the one who's getting teased or bullied, the one who's doing it, or the one who's watching it happen.

Teasing versus Bullying: What's the Difference?

There's a definite difference between bullying and teasing. Bullying (which is sometimes called *harassment*) is when a person or group repeatedly picks on others in order to have power over them or purposely hurt them. Bullying harms not only the person who's being bullied, but those who see it happening, and even the person who's doing the bullying.

Teasing is a different story. Teasing can be annoying and upsetting, but it's not always done with the idea of deliberately hurting another person.

Sometimes teasing is meant to be light and harmless, and if both people involved enjoy it, it can be fun. When teasing is used to have power over others, though, it's no longer teasing—it's bullying. This is what was happening to Eli. Even though no one physically hurt him, the other students exerted cruel power over him. They meant to make him feel unhappy, and they succeeded.

Even if not deliberately meant to harm, teasing becomes a problem when it makes another person feel hurt, put down, or uncomfortable in any way. People who tease often think that the person they're teasing should be able to laugh off their jokes and comments. This is very unfair, because if someone makes you feel bad, you shouldn't have to force yourself to laugh about it or pretend it doesn't hurt.

Think About It

- When is teasing fun? When isn't it?
- What makes the difference?

That goes for teasing from adults, too. No matter who does the teasing, if it feels bad in any way, you have the right to stop it. No one should have to tolerate being the brunt of someone else's jokes or put-downs.

Teasing and put-downs seem to be everywhere these days. In the survey and interviews, kids gave hundreds of comments about being teased and picked on. Here are just a few:

"People tease me because I'm short."

"I get teased because I'm tall."

"I've been picked on because of my ethnicity and weight."

"Kids call me names because I am a good student. Getting A's is a crime these days."

"I got teased because my pants were too tight."

"A kid laughed at me because I don't read well."

"They teased me about stains on my clothes."

"Kids were making fun of my glasses."

"I got picked on by an older girl because her friend said that I was going out with the guy she liked."

There can be a lot of pressure to go along with mean teasing. And, as happened to Eli, too often jokes and put-downs do harm. The truth is, the people who are the coolest don't have to pick on anyone to have a good time or make themselves feel important. People who are really confident inside have the courage to be kind. Like Kayla, who told me, "I see people putting each other down all the time. I don't get involved. What's the point? Just trying to prove you're better than someone is meaningless. It sure doesn't make me feel better if I know I've made somebody else feel worse."

Eight Ways to Stop Teasing

You don't have to stand around and let someone make you feel bad. Here are eight things you can do instead:

1. Try not to let the teasing get the best of you. At least try not to show it. Sometimes people tease to get a rise out of the other person. By reacting, you encourage them to do it more. So ignore it if you can.

2. Agree with the teaser. "Yes I do feel kind of nerd-like today. Funny, yesterday, I felt pretty awesome." Sometimes using humor can get the other person to stop. If you don't react the way the person hopes you will, she or he may give up because there's no payoff.

3. Ask the person to stop. Use an I-message: "I'm not in the mood for this today. Cut it out." (For more on I-messages, see pages 52–56.) Take a look at how Tommy handled it when Len started teasing him about his sneakers:

"Not Funny"

Len: Hey—nice sneakers. Where'd you get them? A garage sale?

Tommy: Not funny.

Len: Aw, lighten up. I was just kidding around.

Tommy: Well, it's not funny to me.

Len: Come on. You have to admit those sneakers are pretty lame.

Tommy: So is putting down what someone else likes.

Len: *(to Tommy)* Okay, sorry. *(under his breath, to himself, "Sheesh—touchy")*

Tommy: *(hears but says nothing, knowing he's made his point)*

4. Walk away. If you ask but the person doesn't stop, walk away with your head held high. Before you go, you might say, "I don't like people making jokes at my expense."

5. Avoid showing hurt or anger. Shouting, crying, or hanging your head will make the problem worse. Remember, people often tease to get a reaction. By reacting in front of someone who picks on you, you give the person too much power. Try to let the bad feelings out privately or with a trusted friend, relative, or teacher.

> ### Real words from the survey
>
> "Kids call me nerd and argue and stuff. I just let them say what they want. If that's the way they feel about it, fine. I just walk away."

6. Talk to someone who can help. If you've tried everything and the teasing continues, definitely talk to someone who cares about you. Talking to someone who's not directly involved can help you think of possible solutions.

7. Rehearse what you'll say next time. Think of an I-message or a snappy comeback—not a mean one—that tells it like it is. Here's what Stephanie did:

> "On my bus there are two boys who sit across from me who are younger than I am, but mean. They say things like, "Even though you're older, we're smarter than you." Most of the time I just ignore them, but sometimes you have to speak up for yourself. One day I decided to outsmart them. I said, "Okay. If you're so smart, what's 8 x 9?" They just looked the other way and got quiet. After that, they left me alone."

Try It

Ask a teacher if the class can have an honest discussion about teasing. Talk about why kids tease, how they feel about it, and what to do about it. See if the class is willing to declare a day without teasing. At the end of the day, discuss what it felt like not to use teasing or put-downs.

Stephanie dealt with her problem by being assertive. She stood up for herself without being nasty or using put-downs. When you're assertive, you're respectful but strong.

8. Stick up for others and ask them to stick up for you. This is one of the most important things you can do. Sticking up for someone else doesn't mean fighting or being nasty. It means speaking your mind firmly but respectfully, like this: "I don't think what you're doing is right. How would you feel if someone treated you that way?" It doesn't matter what the response is. What matters is that you've said something rather than remain silent. The more you and your friends do this, the closer you'll be to getting a handle on mean teasing and put-downs.

Why Do People Bully? Is It Really Such a Big Problem?

People bully because they want power. They often seek out weaker or smaller kids to pick on. Some people who bully have been bullied themselves. The way they handle their built-up anger is by looking for targets to bully. Kids who've observed a lot of bullying might start doing the same to others. It's what they know, something familiar even though it's wrong. And sometimes people who've seen a lot of bullying allow themselves to be bullied even though it feels bad.

Bullying is a huge problem in schools. Consider these findings from several different national studies:

Real words from the survey

"I bully them because they make me mad and I don't see any teachers around."

- 160,000 kids a day skip school for fear of being picked on and bullied.

- Two-thirds of attackers in school shootings reported that they felt bullied, threatened, or injured by others.

- Bullying occurs more often during middle school (grades 6–8) than any other time from elementary through high school.

- 4 out of 10 boys report having been in a physical fight within the last year.

- While boys are far more likely than girls to fight physically, the number of girls who fight physically is rising. Middle school girls are most likely to bully by saying mean things, writing nasty notes, and spreading rumors.

- 60% of people who were considered bullies in grades 6–9 ended up being charged with a crime by age 24.

- Adults who were bullied years ago have higher levels of depression and lower self-esteem than other adults.

There are many more statistics like these, all showing how important it is that kids and adults alike work to stop the problem of bullying.

Self-Check: Are You Bullying or Harassing Anyone?

Some people know they bully—others bully without realizing it. They may not understand how much pain their mean actions can cause. To find out if you do things that could be considered bullying or harassment, take this quick self-test:

Regularly or often . . .

✓ I try to make another person feel bad.

✓ I make fun of a particular person.

✓ I take part in lots of name-calling.

✓ I purposely leave people out.

✓ I cause physical pain to another person.

✓ I threaten someone.

✓ I try to make somebody feel like she or he isn't as good as I am.

✓ I send mean notes, emails, or instant messages about someone else.

✓ I spread rumors about another person.

✓ I try to get others to do any of these things.

Doing any of these on a regular basis is bullying. I know this from my own experience. When I was 13, I used to bully my younger brother. I would call him names, fight with him physically, and try to make him feel bad. Why? Because someone was doing the same thing to me. Of course back then I didn't realize this was the reason I was bullying my brother. But I did know that I got angry a lot. Bullying gave me back a sense of power that was being taken away by the person who was bullying me. In the moments I was doing it, it felt good in a weird way, but afterward I always felt really bad. I knew what I was doing was wrong. Now I wish I would have figured out a lot sooner how to stop both bullying and being bullied.

When you bully, it hurts *you* as well the person you're picking on. Kids who do a lot of bullying form long-term negative habits: They have trouble managing anger and getting along with others. They have broken relationships, too. But you don't have to go down that road.

What to Do If You've Bullied Others

What can you do to break the pattern of bullying for good? Here are six important steps you can take:

1. Admit to yourself what you're doing. It takes a lot of courage to look yourself in the eye and admit you've done something wrong. If you've bullied someone, and you're willing to be honest and face up to it, that's a big move.

2. Make a promise to yourself to stop bullying now. Write it down and put it in a safe place. You might want to share your promise with an adult who you can trust to support you.

3. Make amends. Apologize to the person you've hurt and then do something to make up for your mean actions. For example, you could start including the person in games or activities. Or you could tell your friends that you've gotten to know and like the person and that you're sorry you were so mean. You could also invite the person to your home or offer to help with a tough homework assignment or a tricky sports move. You'll feel better about yourself after making amends.

4. Ask an adult to help you. Talk to your mom, dad, guardian, teacher, or guidance counselor. Or talk to a nurse or doctor, a coach, a youth leader, or someone at your place of worship. If you're not sure what to say, try something like this:

"Do you have a minute? There's something on my mind I need to talk to you about. I've been bullying this kid in my class. I feel bad about it and I want to stop, but I'm not sure how."

Finding the right adult is important. Once you do, this person can help you have the courage to stop the bullying, show respect, make amends, and continue to do the right thing.

Maybe you feel like you want to stop bullying, but you just can't. Sometimes kids bully because they're carrying around bad feelings about other things in their lives—sadness, anger, or worries about friendship problems, girlfriends or boyfriends, parents who fight, family health or money concerns, or abuse. If you have heavy things on your mind and feel bad inside pretty often, you may need help to solve your problems.

Do You Need Help Right Now?

If you need to talk to someone *right now* about bullying or any other serious issues in your life, call the Girls and Boys Town National Hotline: 1-800-448-3000. You can make this toll-free call any time, day or night. A trained professional will be there to talk to you and your call will be confidential. Don't hang up if you have to wait on the line. A real person who cares will be there.

A counselor or youth leader should be able to either help you or refer you to someone who can. Seek out this help so you can stop bullying and start feeling better about yourself. Doing this will help you remember your own dignity and worth as well as the dignity and worth of others.

5. Give yourself credit for the changes you're making. Owning up to what you've done takes a lot of courage. It's is a big deal—for the kid you've bullied and for yourself. You might want to use your notebook to plan the steps you're taking to stop bullying. This will help keep you on track and will remind you of the positive choices you're making.

6. Be part of the bigger solution. Think of ways you can help stop the problem of bullying in your school. Talk to your teacher and other kids about this. Stick up for kids who are being picked on, and ask your friends to do it, too. Remember, bullying will only end when enough people make the decision to stop it. Congratulate yourself for deciding to become one of them.

What to Do If Someone Is Bullying You

If someone is bullying you, you're not alone. Teachers, principals, and researchers know that the majority of kids in schools are being put down, picked on, and worse. Two-thirds of the kids who answered the survey said they had been picked on by others at school or at home. Here are some of their words:

"I was the only white student in my school and because of that I was beaten up every day. I was kicked in my back and eyes. I'm fine now, but I'll remember it forever."

"I am picked on by other kids and it makes me feel scared and frightened."

"My brother used to call me names like fat cow. I would just take it and then cry about it in my room alone."

"My whole life I've been called four-eyes, crave-eyes, and much more."

"People spit food at my friends and me."

"These girls would harass my friends and me constantly. On the Internet they would threaten to kill us."

Did you know that a recent Miss America, Erika Harold, was bullied mercilessly as a kid? It began in ninth grade with girls who were once her friends. For reasons Erika still doesn't understand, they turned on her. Before she knew it, everyone else started joining in. Students picked on her for everything imaginable: for raising her hand, for the way she looked, and for her multiracial background. The kids used to write down all the things she did that they considered "uncool" and then read their list out loud at the end of class. The bullying continued out of school, too. Erika's house was even vandalized.

The worst blow was to Erika's self-esteem. "When day in and day out people pick on everything about you, it makes you question yourself," she said. She would try to hold in her feelings when she was at school, but every day she would go home and cry. Luckily, Erika had supportive parents who were able to help her withstand the harassment she was experiencing and to realize it wasn't her fault. That's how she was able to heal.

As a result of her experiences, Erika Harold has put together an anti-bullying campaign. She regularly speaks to students and teachers about this problem. She says: "If Miss America has been harassed, it can happen to anyone. You don't have to be ashamed if it's happening to you." Erika tells students to be proud of their own individuality, not to apologize for who they are. And she encourages them not to let bullies keep control, explaining, "I learned that you can gain power from the things you have suffered through. You can use it to change things."

You deserve respect simply for being you. That's enough. *Every* person is worthy of respect, and there is no one who has the right to take that away from you. The trouble is that when you constantly face put-downs and violence, it tears away at your self-esteem. You begin to lose sight of all that you are capable of and all you have to contribute, and you start to doubt yourself. But it doesn't have to stay that way.

Know That You Have Worth and Value

Kids who are bullied tend to think they're being picked on because there's something wrong with them. This is absolutely not true. People who bully are looking for an available target, so they latch on to the next convenient person they feel they can have power over. You just happen to be that person, and when it isn't you, it's going to be someone else. So if you're feeling that the bullying is somehow your fault, let go of that idea. It's not your fault. No one deserves to be bullied. Period.

Too often kids who are bullied keep the problem inside because they feel embarrassed or ashamed. Doing this only makes it worse. Shame and silence can make you forget the power you have inside. Always remember that you have worth and value. You don't have to be thin, cool, smart, white, black, well-dressed, free of handicaps, or good in sports to be worthy of respect. Your uniqueness is what makes you special. Unfortunately there are too many kids who believe that the only way to be popular is to dress, talk, eat, act, and look like everyone else. Well, they've got it backward. The most interesting people in life are the ones who don't fit into any particular mold. So know that you don't have to let anyone else's words or actions make you feel less than you are.

Prepare Yourself

Working on your self-esteem and self-confidence will help you deal with bullying from a place of strength. And being strong outside is as important as feeling strong inside. You can prepare yourself to deal with bullying so you're able to take strong, smart action when it happens.

Have you ever heard the saying "There's strength in numbers"? People who bully often look for kids who are alone. By finding people to hang out with, you can help keep yourself from being approached by a bully in the first place. Another strong move is to rehearse ways to respond to bullying. It's hard to think of what to say on the spot when someone's being mean to you. Practicing ahead of time, in front of a mirror or with another person, really helps. Four key things to rehearse are assertive words, a steady voice, eye contact, and strong body posture.

Assertive words:

- "Don't talk to me that way. Do you understand?"

- "I totally disagree."

- "I'm not going to listen to this stuff."

- "I'm not going to take this."

- "Your words are meaningless to me."

- "It seems like you're enjoying trying to make me feel bad, but it's not working."

- "Stop it."

Steady voice: Work on keeping your voice firm and strong without shouting. You want your tone of voice to communicate that you're in control (even if you don't feel that way inside). The more you practice and use an assertive voice, the more in charge you'll feel.

Eye contact: It's important to look directly at the person when you speak. Looking down or away removes the power of your words.

Body posture: Stand straight. Keep your chin high and your shoulders square. This sends a message of strength and confidence.

> ### Try It
>
> In front of the mirror, practice all four parts of your response: words, tone of voice, eye contact, and posture. Rehearsing this will help you to experience a shift inside toward greater confidence.

Don't forget to breathe! When you're frightened or nervous, your breathing becomes shallow, making you more frightened or nervous. You can reverse this by practicing the deep abdominal breathing you read about in Step 5 (pages 71–72). The more you use deep breathing, the more calm and in control you'll feel when you face the person who's been bullying you.

Mental rehearsal will also help "reprogram" your brain from fear to strength. Every night before you go to sleep and each morning when you wake up, take a few deep abdominal breaths. Then picture yourself successfully dealing with the person who's bullying you. In your mind, imagine yourself standing and *feeling* brave and strong. See your eyes looking straight into the other person's. Hear your voice saying assertive words with firm confidence. Then watch yourself walk away strong and proud.

Keep Yourself Safe

If you're in danger of being physically harmed, the smart move is to keep yourself safe. Here are ways to gain control and exit a dangerous situation:

- Stand up straight, look the person in the eye, and say in a firm, confident voice, "Leave me alone!" Then walk away quickly and calmly.

- Shout "Cut it out!" as loudly as you can.

- Join a group of people nearby so you're not alone.

- If you're in real danger—for example, if you're facing a gang of bullies—run as fast as you can to a safe place. At other times, it might be better to stand your ground and stick up for yourself. Trust your instincts.

One of the main sources of violence among kids and teens is gang activity. Gangs put kids on a path of constant conflict, often leading to prison and death. Some of the students I surveyed and interviewed were worried about pressure from gangs. Here's important advice from gang expert Dominick Cicala who has dealt with gangs and gang members for decades:

- If you're asked to join, say no, but say it respectfully.

- Don't show interest. Gang members usually look for people who want to join. Kids who aren't interested are often left alone.

- Don't get into conversations with gang members. If someone approaches you, keep moving and get yourself away as quickly as possible. Use an excuse, even one like, "I have to go to the bathroom."

- If you pass the same corner every day where you get pressured, think about taking a different route.

- If you're already involved in a gang, get yourself out. It's possible to do this. According to Dominick Cicala, 7 out of 10 gang members leave within a year. If you stay in a gang, you can end up in prison for life or you can lose your life.

- Avoid people and places associated with the gang. Move in with another relative if you need to.

> "We are all born with freedom, but I lost mine when I lost my sense of responsibility.
> I didn't like rules, and that's how I ended up in prison. My advice to all kids:
> Don't get involved in something that can lead to prison and death.
> If you want to be in a group, do something positive."
> "José," a former gang member now in jail

Reach Out for Help

You may not always be able to deal with problems like gangs and bullying by yourself. Erika Harold turned both to her own inner power and to her parents to cope with being bullied. If someone is bullying you, talk to a parent or guardian, teacher, guidance counselor, principal, coach, youth leader, or good friend about what's going on. If the person you first talk to doesn't know how to solve the problem, ask for help finding someone who does.

"Yes, But" Questions

"Yes, but what if someone hurts me and they threaten to do it again if I tell?" They're threatening you because they're afraid of getting in trouble. When adults do this it's called blackmail, and it's illegal. If someone hurts you or threatens your safety in any way, don't remain silent. Talk to a trusted adult as quickly as possible.

"Yes, but what if they tell me they're going to wait for me off the school grounds?" All the more reason to tell an adult. Talk to a teacher or guidance counselor. School systems have rules in place to protect you in school and on the way home. By remaining silent, you put yourself at greater risk. Speak up, speak out, and know that there are people who will help protect you. Don't try to do it alone. Also, don't be afraid to let your local police know if someone has threatened to harm you or someone you care about.

"Yes, but what if telling makes it worse?" Then it's time for a family adult to sit down with the principal. Your school has an obligation to keep you safe. Your parent or guardian can also ask for a meeting with the super-

intendent of schools. Keep reaching out until you get results. This is your best guarantee of protection. Don't allow yourself to be defeated by someone else's threats.

"Yes, but kids will accuse me of tattling." Tell an adult anyway, and explain this part of it, too. Asking for help is a lot different from tattling. You can't allow yourself to be put in a position of being unsafe. Try your best to ignore negative comments unless you feel completely overwhelmed by them. If that happens, ask your counselor to step in. By doing this, you will also help protect other kids who are being picked on.

"Yes, but what if it's a member of my group who's threatening me, and I feel like I need to be loyal?" Ask yourself this: If your best friend was being threatened, what advice would you offer? You'd probably be more concerned about your friend's safety than group loyalty. And you'd be right. Safety comes first. So if the same thing is happening to you, you need to treat yourself like you would a good friend. Another question: If someone in your group is threatening or hurting you, do you really want to be loyal to this person?

"Yes, but what if I'm too scared to tell anyone I'm being picked on?" You can either give in to the fear and continue being picked on, or do something about it and end the problem. You can also ask adults at your school to start addressing the issue of fights and bullying in general. By coming forward you might be able to help other kids in this situation. Start building a network of kids and teachers who are willing to work on this. Then you won't feel so alone.

Another option is to talk to an adult about how you can confront the person who's picking on you. Decide what to say and role-play it first for practice. If this assertive approach doesn't work, you have two choices—have an adult mediate, or have the adult talk to the person who's picking on you. With any of these choices, you're not giving in to the fear.

"Yes, but I got bullied by these girls who I thought were my friends. They did a three-way phone call without my knowing it. One of them called me. She started to talk about another girl in the group and got me to talk about her, too. I didn't know it, but the girl was listening in. Now the whole group is against me. What should I do?" Three-way phone calls are a form of bullying that no one should ever tolerate. You need to take action. Here's what you can do:

- Confront the girl who set you up and tell her how it felt to be betrayed. If you can't do this by yourself, ask your guidance counselor for help.

- Take responsibility if you did something that made your friends mad enough to want to hurt you in such a cruel way. No one deserves to be treated like you were, but you need to see if there was a role you played in provoking what happened.

- Make amends to the girl who you said bad things about. Apologize and consider making a promise not to talk about her again.

- Expand your friendships so that you have choices of other people to hang out with. Maybe these girls don't deserve your loyalty.

Bullying and Sexual Harassment

You've probably heard of *sexual harassment*. It refers to teasing, put-downs, threats, and other kinds of bullying focused on sex and sexuality, and it's a big

Facts

- In a national U.S. survey, 4 out of 5 students said they had experienced some kind of sexual harassment at school.

- More than 1 in 4 students say they are often sexually harassed.

- One study found that 97% of teens reported regularly hearing anti-gay comments from their classmates at school.

part of bullying in middle school and high school. It hurts everyone and leads to lots of conflicts.

Something that came up several times in the surveys and interviews was the use of the word *gay* as a put-down. One student who talked about this said, "It's unbelievable the way people use the word *gay*. It definitely shouldn't be something people are prejudiced about. But they are. It's awful the way people make fun of other people because they're different. But everybody's different. What would the world be if everyone was the same?"

Some people are gay. Some people are also short, tall, black, or white. No one has the right to use what someone *is* as a slur. Think about it, and think of all the things you are. Ask yourself how you would feel if someone used one of those things—your sex, color, religion, cultural background, financial status, size, shape, health, intelligence—as a slur on a regular basis. Maybe someone does put you down based on one of these things. Then you know how terrible it feels. *Gay* is just another way people can be, and using this as a put-down is not only wrong, it's downright damaging.

What You Can Do About Sexual Harassment

Here's how *you* can help prevent this cruel form of bullying:

DON'T . . .

- Use a label like *gay* or *lesbian* as a put-down.

- Call people names like "fag," "wuss," or "slut."

- Make sexual jokes or comments about body parts.

- Touch, grab, or yank at people's clothing.

- Use obscene hand movements or sounds.

- Spread sexual gossip or write sexual notes.

- Laugh or remain silent when others do these things.

DO . . .

- Speak up when other people do these things. Let them know it's wrong. Have the courage not to go along with the crowd.

- Get help from a trusted adult if you are the person being harassed.

- Report sexual harassment to the principal.

- Talk with other kids, teachers, and counselors about the harm it does.

Choose to Be a Peacemaker

One of the kids I interviewed for this book told me: "Kids are mean to each other because they want to be better than everybody else. We can change this by making every person feel like they mean something in the world."

Your life means something in this world. In fact, it means a lot. Every word you speak and every action you take counts. By treating yourself and others with respect, you make the world a little kinder, a little safer, and a little more peaceful. You have the capacity to choose to do this every day of your life.

Build Yourself Up from the Inside Out

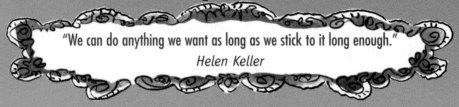

"We can do anything we want as long as we stick to it long enough."
Helen Keller

In this chapter you'll discover:

- a day-by-day action plan to help you grow as a conflict solver
- more strategies for handling your toughest challenges
- ideas for staying focused so you can stick with your commitment to peacemaking

So now you have all this information about resolving conflicts and becoming a peacemaker. How do you put it all into practice? And how do you keep at it when the going gets tough? Maybe you need a little more support in strengthening your confidence and courage. You may also find it helpful to have a clear-cut plan you can use to keep focused on staying cool, feeling strong and in control, and sticking with your commitment to conflict solving. This chapter will give you both of those things: first, a daily action plan that will help you use the skills in this book; then, more ideas for building and sustaining the "muscles" that will support you in being a peaceful person.

Follow a Day-by-Day Plan

Maybe you've heard the expression "One day at a time." You'll need time to put into practice the many strategies you've read about. A daily action plan will break down everything into doable parts so you can focus on one step at a time. Here's how: Copy and use the "Conflict Solver's Action Plan" on pages 127–133 as your guide. Each page has empowerment statements and actions you can take to get along better with people and feel good about yourself.

Put the pages of the plan in the top drawer of your dresser. Each day, take out one page. Start with Day 1 and do three things:

- Read the empowerment statement to encourage yourself and begin your day on a positive note.

- Repeat the empowerment statement as you're getting ready for the day. (Repeat it later on, too.)

- Read the "Actions for Today." Choose at least one action to take during this day.

Picture this day being a really good one, and the action plan being part of making it happen. Your action plan will put you in charge of yourself. Instead of letting moods, disappointments, challenges, or other people decide what kind of day it will be, *you* get to create the kind of day you want. If challenges, problems, or disappointments come up, you'll be ready to deal with them from a positive and strong state of mind.

Each day, do another page. When you finish with Day 7, start over with Day 1. This way, every day you'll have a plan that will help you fully use the power you have to create more peace in yourself and in your life.

Strengthen Your Courage Muscle

Earlier you read about how vital your courage muscle is when it comes to being a conflict solver. Courage leads to confidence that lets you choose to do the right thing in tough situations. You've learned lots of ways to build your courage muscle, and a super-important one is to stick up for others either by yourself or with a friend. Each time you do this you'll feel stronger, be stronger, and have more self-respect—regardless of what others have to say. Yes, some kids might ignore your words or tell you to mind your own business. But something inside them will notice that *you* have the courage to stand up for another person. By defending someone who's being picked on, you might help other people do the same. Your example makes a difference.

Read these words of courage from two middle school kids:

"These kids were making fun of my friend. They were calling him names and swearing at him. He just sat there and tried to think of something to say, but they kept on making fun of him. He looked like he was going to cry. I didn't want to just stand there while they hurt him like that. Finally I told the kids to leave him alone and go away. I looked right at them and used a serious tone. They listened to me and stopped picking on him. My friend thanked me. I was glad I did it."

"I stuck up for this kid who people were always picking on. He had huge teeth and a small jaw, and he had trouble learning some stuff at school. He wanted to play basketball, and he was good at it, too. But no one wanted him on their team. So I said, 'He has as much right to play as you do. You're only leaving him out because he's different. You're being prejudiced.' I couldn't stay quiet and let them treat him that way."

Visualize It

Close your eyes, breathe deeply, and bring your confident self (see page 90) into your mind. Visualize your confident self standing tall and feeling brave. Now see yourself sticking up for someone who could use some help. Picture doing this on your own or by asking some friends to join you. Imagine your words and actions helping the other person. Notice the self-respect you feel as a result. Let this fill your mind and body.

Standing up for someone else is the highest form of courage there is. Each time you do this, your courage muscle strengthens and makes room for more courage to come in.

A powerful story of courage comes from a boy at a large city high school. He told how, in the days following September 11, 2001, the kids of Middle Eastern descent were getting picked on by students from other ethnic groups. This boy put the word out to all his friends not to let any of the Middle Eastern kids walk alone in the halls. After that, when someone would make remarks about the Middle Eastern kids' race or religion or blame them for what happened on 9/11, the person who was walking by their side would say something like this: "How would you feel if someone from your background blew up the World Trade Center? This kid had nothing to do with it and you need to understand how bad your comment is making him feel." Before long, a lot of the harassment stopped.

One person's courage can really have a big impact! Even if you feel nervous when you're sticking up for someone else, your courage muscle will still be growing.

Strengthen Your Forgiveness Muscle

The sixth Win/Win Guideline is to affirm, forgive, thank, or apologize to each other. By the time you've worked through all of the guidelines, affirming, thanking the other person, or even apologizing might feel pretty natural. But kids and adults often say that really forgiving the other person can be a very tough challenge. Sometimes we feel that we were really right and the other person was really wrong. At other times we stay angry or resentful because the hurt's still there. Part of us may want to punish the person who made us feel bad. It's human nature to hold a grudge from time to time. The trouble is, when we do, it usually makes things worse. Holding onto anger and resentment hurts *us* most. It can actually affect our emotional and physical health, keeping us stressed, angry, and unhappy. No person is worth getting sick over, especially when *you're* the one who ends up suffering. But when you're able to really forgive someone else, you can shed those bad feelings. Studies have shown that when people choose to forgive, they become more hopeful, more self-confident, and healthier.

Forgiving doesn't mean you have to accept what's unacceptable or act like it's okay. What it does mean is that you're willing to let go of the resentment you've been holding onto. It's saying to yourself, "I won't let this anger take up space in my brain anymore."

> **Talk About It**
>
> Is there a person or group of people in your school who are always being picked on? Talk to your friends and see if you can figure out a way to help. Try talking to some teachers about this, too. Now put your plan into action.

> "Holding onto resentment is like drinking poison and hoping it will kill your enemy."
> *Nelson Mandela*

You might feel like you have no control over feelings of anger and resentment. But in reality, you do—you have it within you to choose forgiveness instead. Here's a powerful exercise that can help you let go and forgive. It comes from Dr. Fred Luskin, a top expert on forgiveness:

1. Close your eyes and picture the person who hurt or angered you. Let all your bad feelings come up. Notice what happens in your body.

2. Now take five slow, deep abdominal breaths. By focusing on your breathing, let go of the image of the person who hurt you. If your mind returns to the person, gently pull the focus back to the rhythm of the air going in and out of your nostrils.

3. With your eyes still closed, bring into your mind an image of someone you love very much, or a place that's very peaceful. Allow yourself to be flooded with good feelings as you focus on this person or place. Imagine these good feelings surrounding your heart. Now allow the feelings to flow into your heart and soothe you.

4. Keep breathing the good feelings into your heart. As you do, allow the picture of the person who hurt you back into your mind. Picture the good feelings in your heart calming you, protecting you from the bad feelings this person usually brings out. Imagine the person having no power over you.

Try It

Remember the secret of 5/25? Do the forgiveness exercise for the next 25 days. Also use it at any other time you think of the person who hurt you. Slowly, it will begin to change your mental and physical reactions. When this happens, the resentment will start to dissolve.

Writing about the situation is another way you can work toward forgiving someone. In your notebook, answer these questions:

- What did the person do to upset you?

- Why do you think you're holding onto your anger toward the person?

- How do you feel when you see the person?

- How might you feel if you were able to forgive the person?

- Once you're ready to forgive, what do you need to say or do so you both know that you've truly forgiven the person?

Forgiving doesn't mean forgetting what someone did, or letting yourself be hurt again. It means deciding to let go of the anger you've been carrying around. The situation is over and done with. Now you leave it in the past.

Observe Yourself

Maybe you're handling conflict pretty well a lot of the time, but sometimes your strong feelings still take over. Here's a trick that might help you handle anger, hurt, fear, and any bad feeling that tends to get the best of you. Imagine "stepping out of yourself" and watching you. It may sound a little strange, but it can work. Observing yourself from the outside lets you notice your mood as if it belonged to someone else. Picture yourself stepping out of you and standing at the side of the room. Imagine your "observer self" watching you. Your observer self lets you simply notice what's going on without getting hooked. It's one of the keys to personal power.

Try this little experiment: Look in a mirror. Invite your observer self to step out of you and notice what you're thinking. Look at your face. Maybe your observer self is watching you as you think something like, "Nice zit," or "I hate these braces!" Or maybe it's noticing you thinking, "Not bad," or "Pretty cute." Whatever your mind is thinking, your observer self can look on and just notice instead of being affected by it.

This same observer self can help you step away from negative emotions. Next time you're upset about something, invite your observer self to step outside of you and watch what's going on. It might go something like this, "Hmm, I'm noticing myself feeling pretty upset right now. I'm noticing myself crying a few tears. I'm noticing myself thinking about what happened today and feeling really bad. Now I'm noticing myself feeling a little better. Hmm, I'm noticing myself wanting to get up and have a snack. How about that!"

Your observer self can give you enough detachment that your bad feelings can start to loosen their grip. It allows you to feel what you feel without getting carried away by destructive thoughts that might otherwise escalate and take over. Try calling on your observer self the next time you're in a bad mood. Get comfortable using this technique, and then try it when you're in a conflict and need some extra help staying cool and calm.

Think About It

Think of someone you really admire. What qualities do you admire in this person? Now think about a tricky conflict situation you want to deal with in a better way. What would the person you admire do in the same situation? Try it next time and see if it helps.

Observe Others

Another way to boost your conflict-solving skills is to find role models. Maybe you remember that Lara did this in when she watched her friend Saj to see how he listened so well (see page 40). A role model can help with other aspects of conflict solving, too. Do you know someone who handles conflicts really well? Someone who is often respectful, kind, and fair? Maybe you have a friend like this. Maybe it's one of your teachers or a relative.

Let this person be a role model in your mind. For example, your Uncle Jim might be someone you totally admire because he's strong and kind at the same time. So the next time your stepbrother goes in your room without your permission, imagine what Uncle Jim would do if it were *his* room. Picture yourself doing what Uncle Jim would do. Then go ahead and do it. Maybe you think Uncle Jim would calm down first, gather his thoughts, plan what he's going to say, and then say something like this:

"I know you like to be in here. But remember, it IS my room, and it's important to me that you ask before coming in. I promise I'll do the same for you."

Believe in Yourself

Lots of kids in the survey and interviews admitted that worries about being accepted by others kept them from making peace. They felt pressured to go along with what other kids in their group did. One boy said, "You have to watch yourself so you don't end up on the outside." Maybe you feel this way, too. Or maybe you're like some other students who said they don't pay attention to what the popular kids, or the cool kids, or any other kids thought. They understand that having self-respect is the key to feeling good about themselves and making good choices when it comes to conflict. Read the words of one of these kids, a sixth-grader named Briana:

"When I see people picking on other kids, I usually ask if they would like it if someone picked on them. And I remind them that what they're doing hurts the person's feelings. A lot of times, they'll stop. Or if they make comments about kids who come from different countries, I'll say, 'You shouldn't make fun of people just because of their clothes or skin color. It doesn't matter what people look like on the outside. We're all the same on the inside. Everyone has feelings.'

"If someone says mean things to me, I give them an I-message, or I walk away and pretend I didn't hear. Things like that don't bother me. It doesn't matter what they think. It's what I think that matters most."

It would be terrific if someone could bottle up Briana's courage and self-confidence to give to people everywhere. Briana is deeply aware of her own self-worth, so speaking up or tuning out when she needs to isn't a chore. I hope you feel like Briana does. But maybe you're not there yet. If you want to feel like this but still struggle because it's hard to take a stand, to be on the outside, or to take pride in being different, be patient with yourself.

What qualities do you admire in other people? Looks, popularity, style, brains, kindness, honesty, fairness, and acceptance? The first three qualities are easy to envy from afar, but they don't guarantee self-confidence. In fact, some of the most insecure people try to cover up their insecurity by having trendy clothes and being the center of the attention.

Real words from the survey

"The people I usually see having conflicts are ones who seem insecure and feel the need to be higher than they really are, no matter whether it's a geek or jock or valley girl."

The people who actually feel best about themselves feel good from the inside out. They don't need the external stuff because they respect who they are, take pride in their unique talents, and have good relationships with their families and friends. They might not be part of the popular or cool group at all. Or they might spend time in different groups depending on what they want to do. Being part of a clique or group simply doesn't matter that much to them. They have what they need on the inside and they can depend on themselves to be kind, honest, caring, and decent. That's how self-respect grows. It's not about who you hang out with or what you look like on the outside. And it's not gained by putting others down.

If you've been doing many of the exercises in the chapters so far, you're already on your way to building more and more confidence and self-respect. Keep at it, and keep working at all the things you've been learning in this book. Just like anything else worth accomplishing, becoming a conflict solver takes time and patience. Think of other challenges you've worked hard at, like a sport, a tough subject, or a musical instrument. It probably took effort and commitment to improve your performance. Becoming a more peaceful person inside and out will take the same kind of perseverance. Use the daily action plan to build the skills and strategies that can help you harness your personal power and keep growing as a peacemaker. Everyplace you go offers an opportunity to do so—home, school, the bus, the playing field, the mall, and your neighborhood. Remember, Team Earth needs you to increase the peace. You've got the power. Use it!

Conflict Solver's Action Plan
Day 1: Keep an open mind.

> ## Today's empowerment statement:
>
> I feel good on the inside when I choose
> the balcony over the basement.

Actions I can take today:

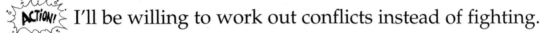 I'll be willing to work out conflicts instead of fighting.

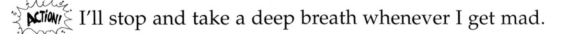 I'll stop and take a deep breath whenever I get mad.

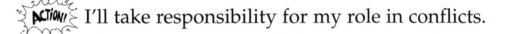 I'll take responsibility for my role in conflicts.

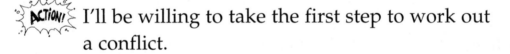 I'll be willing to take the first step to work out
a conflict.

I'll resist the urge to blame.

CONFLICT SOLVER'S ACTION PLAN
Day 2: Choose to solve conflicts.

> ### Today's empowerment statement:
>
> My words and actions are respectful.

Actions I can take today:

 I'll use a calming statement when I feel upset, angry, or tense.

 I'll stand up for myself without going on the attack.

 I'll act brave, strong, and respectful even if my feelings pull me in another direction.

 I'll stay in the balcony even when others are in the basement.

CONFLICT SOLVER'S ACTION PLAN
Day 3: Become a better listener.

Today's empowerment statement:

Listening helps me get along better
with the people in my life.

Actions I can take today:

ACTION! I'll focus on the speaker.

ACTION! I'll resist the urge to interrupt or to let my mind
drift off when someone is speaking.

ACTION! I'll use reflective listening to understand another
person's feelings and point of view.

ACTION! I'll focus on listening if I'm in a conflict with someone.

Conflict Solver's Action Plan
Day 4: Use Win/Win Guidelines.

Today's empowerment statement:

I can resolve conflicts peacefully.

Actions I can take today:

ACTION! I'll cool off so I can talk things over respectfully.

ACTION! I'll use I-messages to express my point of view.

ACTION! I'll compromise and seek solutions.

ACTION! I'll remember to attack the problem, not the person.

ACTION! I'll choose working it out over fighting it out.

CONFLICT SOLVER'S ACTION PLAN

Day 5: Manage anger.

Today's empowerment statement:

I have the power to control my anger.

Actions I can take today:

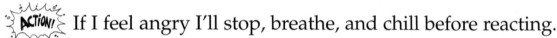 If I feel angry I'll stop, breathe, and chill before reacting.

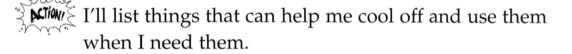 I'll list things that can help me cool off and use them when I need them.

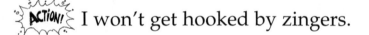 I won't get hooked by zingers.

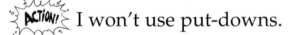 I won't use put-downs.

 I'll seek an adult's help with anger if I need to.

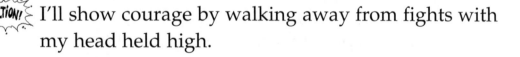 I'll show courage by walking away from fights with my head held high.

CONFLICT SOLVER'S ACTION PLAN
Day 6: Manage stress.

Today's empowerment statement:

I have what I need inside to keep cool and calm.

Actions I can take today:

ACTION! I'll start my day with deep breathing and visualize my confident self.

ACTION! I'll use my empowerment statement throughout the day.

ACTION! I'll de-stress in healthy ways.

ACTION! I'll spend time with someone who cares about me.

ACTION! I'll cut back on TV and video games.

ACTION! I'll end my day with a calming activity like deep breathing, yoga, or meditation.

Conflict Solver's Action Plan
Day 7: Be smart about bullying.

Today's empowerment statement:

I can be strong and kind at the same time.

Actions I can take today:

 I'll take responsibility and make amends if I have hurt anyone in the past.

 I'll stop myself immediately from hurting someone physically or with my words.

 I'll get help or act assertively if someone tries to bully me.

 I'll find an adult who can help me deal with problems I can't solve on my own.

 I'll stick up for someone who's being teased, picked on, put down, or bullied.

 I'll ask my friend to stick up for someone who's being bullied, too.

Resources for You

Books

Hot Stuff to Help Kids Chill Out: The Anger Management Book by Jerry Wilde (Richmond, IN: LGR Publishing, 1997). This book offers unique ideas for managing anger rather than being controlled by it.

How to Handle Bullies, Teasers and Other Meanies: A Book That Takes the Nuisance Out of Name Calling and Other Nonsense by Kate Cohen-Posey (Highland City, FL: Rainbow Books, 1995). Provides information on what makes bullies and teasers tick, how to handle bullies, how to deal with prejudice, and how to defend oneself when being teased or insulted.

How to Take the Grrrr Out of Anger by Elizabeth Verdick and Marjorie Lisovskis (Minneapolis: Free Spirit Publishing, 2003). Filled with lots of advice and humor, this book will help you understand anger—what it is, what it does, where it comes from, how it feels—and how to handle it in healthy, positive ways.

More Hot Stuff to Help Kids Chill Out: The Anger and Stress Management Book by Jerry Wilde (Richmond, IN: LGR Publishing, 2001). This follow-up to the original *Hot Stuff* provides more ideas for how to cope with anger and hostility and also contains information on managing stress, which is an important part of any anger-management program.

The 7 Habits of Highly Effective Teens by Sean Covey (New York: Simon and Schuster, 1998). This is a step-by-step guide to improving self-image, building friendships, dealing with peer pressure, getting along with their parents, and much more. The book includes a chapter on the benefits of being a good listener.

Stick Up for Yourself! Every Kid's Guide to Personal Power and Positive Self-Esteem by Gershen Kaufman, Lev Raphael, and Pamela Espeland (Minneapolis: Free Spirit Publishing, 1999). Read this book to learn more ways to be brave and strong and how to use "personal power" responsibly in your relationships with other kids and adults.

Stress Can Really Get on Your Nerves by Trevor Romain and Elizabeth Verdick (Minneapolis: Free Spirit Publishing, 2000). If stress is a big issue in your life, you might want to check out this funny but helpful book for more information about where stress comes from and how to cope.

Understanding the Human Volcano: What Teens Can Do About Violence by Earl Hipp (Center City, MN: Hazelden Publishing and Educational Services, 2000). Young people today (and their parents) feel a growing concern for their safety and have some anxiety about their classmates and sense of security. Speaking directly, frankly, and compassionately, the author helps young people cope in an increasingly violent and less secure world and shows them how to do something about violence.

Why Is Everybody Always Picking on Me? by Terrence Webster-Doyle (New York: Weatherhill, 2000). This book discusses bullies and victims and teaches how *not* to be either one. Stories, role plays, and questions help you learn how to solve your conflicts nonviolently.

Why Is Everybody Always Picking on Us? Understanding the Roots of Prejudice by Terrence Webster-Doyle (New York: Weatherhill, 2000). Learn where prejudice begins, how it is created, how it is perpetuated, and how it can be resolved. This book looks at stereotypes, bigotry, discrimination, scapegoating, racism, and more.

Yoga for Teens: How to Improve Your Fitness, Confidence, Appearance, and Health— and Have Fun Doing It! by Thia Luby (Santa Fe, NM: Clear Light, 2000). Whether you're a beginner or have some experience with yoga, this inspiring book will show you plenty of yoga poses you can do alone, with a partner, or in a group.

Web Sites

Bullying.org

Bullying.org is an international anti-bullying resource that helps people understand that they're not alone in being bullied, being bullied is not their fault, and there are many positive alternatives to dealing with bullying. See pictures and read stories and poems about bullying from kids around the world. You can comment on the submissions and read others' comments, too.

It's My Life • *pbskids.org/itsmylife*

It's My Life deals with life and everyday stuff—stuff that other kids and teens also have gone through. You'll find articles, kids' stories, games and activities, quizzes and polls, video clips of other kids talking about their feelings and experiences, and advice from older kids and experts on sibling rivalry, friends fighting, bullies, anger management, and more. You can contribute your own comments and questions.

Kids Health • *KidsHealth.org*

KidsHealth has separate areas for kids, teens, and parents—each full of features, articles, animations, games, and resources on all sorts of topics. Type the word *bully* in the search box to find lots of information on bullying, peer pressure, good sportsmanship, and more.

This is the survey I sent to middle school students. You can photocopy it for personal or classroom use. If this book is from the library, please don't write in it.

WORKING OUT CONFLICTS SURVEY

Your age:	Are you a: (circle one) boy girl		
Where you live: (circle one)	Urban Area	Suburb	Small Town Rural Area

1. How often do you see kids having conflicts such as arguments or fights? (circle one)

Often
(several times a day)

Sometimes
(at least once a day)

Not very often
(less than once a day)

2. How often do YOU have conflicts such as arguments or fights? (circle one)

Often
(several times a day)

Sometimes
(at least once a day)

Not very often
(less than once a day)

3. Have you ever been picked on by other kids? What happened, and what did you do about it? (explain in as much detail as possible)_____

_____

_____

4. How do you feel when kids have conflicts? (explain)_____

_____

_____

5. Who do you usually see having conflicts?_____

_____

6. What do kids usually do when they have a conflict or trouble with someone?

_____

_____

7. What do YOU usually do when you have a conflict with someone? _____

_____

_____

more ⟶

8. Which best states how you feel? (please check any that apply)

❑ I think I work out problems with people pretty well.

❑ I wish I was better at working out problems with others.

❑ I'm not very good at working out problems with others.

❑ I'd like to learn more about working out problems with others.

9. What three things do you or your friends or siblings have the most conflicts about?

_____

_____

10. What, if anything, does your school do to help kids to solve problems or conflicts peacefully? For example, do they have a peer mediation program? _____

_____

_____

11. Do you think learning how to resolve conflicts peacefully is important? Why or why not? _____

_____

12. What do you most want to learn about resolving conflicts? _____

_____

_____

13. On a scale of 1–10, how mean do you think kids generally are to each other? Please put an X on the scale below.

1	2	3	4	5	6	7	8	9	10

not mean at all   the meanest it's possible to be

14. How do you think we can get kids to stop being mean to each other? _____

_____

_____

References

Chapter 2

The "Facts" on page 30 are from "Youth and Violence: Students Speak Out for a More Civil Society," by Ellen Galinsky and Kimberlee Salmond (Families and Work Institute and The Colorado Trust, 2002).

Chapter 4

The "Win/Win Guidelines," first cited on page 50, are adapted from *Learning the Skills of Peacemaking* (revised edition), by Naomi Drew (Torrance, CA: Jalmar Press, 1995). Used with permission.

Chapter 6

The "Fact" on page 94 is from "Youth and Violence: Students Speak Out for a More Civil Society," by Ellen Galinsky and Kimberlee Salmond (Families and Work Institute and The Colorado Trust, 2002).

The "Fact" on page 98 is from "Grounded for Life: Teens Are Turning to Yoga to Find Self-Acceptance," by Colleen Morton Busch, *Yoga Journal* (August 2003).

Chapter 7

The statistics in "Why Do People Bully? Is It Really Such a Big Problem?" on pages 104–105 are from:

"Words That Wound," by Kathleen Vail, *The American School Board Journal* (September 1999): pp. 37–40; "Gunman in School Attacks Sought Revenge, Revealed Plans," by Jessica Portner, *Education Week* (October 25, 2000); "Addressing the Problem of Juvenile Bullying," by Nels Ericson, Office of Juvenile Justice and Delinquency Prevention (June 2001); "Youth Risk Behavior Surveillance System Summary" (Washington, DC: U.S. Department of Health and Human Services, 1999); "Girls Just Want to Be Mean," by Margaret Talbot, *The New York Times Magazine* (February 24, 2002): p. 26; "Preventing and

Reducing Social Aggression Among Girls," by Marion K. Underwood, *The Brown University Child and Adolescent Behavior Letter* (December 2003): p. 1; *Bullying at School: What We Know and What We Can Do* by Dan Olweus (Cambridge, MA: Blackwell, 1994); "Health Consequences of Bullying and Its Prevention in Schools," by Ken Rigby in *Peer Harassment in School: The Plight of the Vulnerable and Victimized* edited by Jaana Juvonen and Sandra Graham (New York: Guilford Press, 2001).

Erika Harold's quotes on page 109 are from a speech she gave on March 17, 2003, at Rutgers University.

In the "Keep Yourself Safe" section on page 112, the list of ways to exit a dangerous situation are adapted from *The Bully Free Classroom* by Alan L. Beane (Minneapolis: Free Spirit Publishing, 1999): pp. 42–43. Used with permission.

The advice on pages 112–113 about staying out of gangs is from a phone interview with Dominick Cicala (December 2003).

The "Facts" on page 116 are from *Hostile Hallways: Bullying, Teasing, and Sexual Harassment in School* (Washington, DC: American Association of University Women Educational Foundation, 2001), and *Making Schools Safe for Gay and Lesbian Youth* (Boston: Governor's Commission on Gay and Lesbian Youth, 1999).

Chapter 8

The forgiveness exercise on page 122 is from Dr. Fred Luskin, Director of the Stanford Forgiveness Projects and author of *Forgive for Good*. Used with permission.

Index

Page numbers in **bold** indicate reproducibles.

About the Author

Naomi Drew, M.A., is a well-known expert on conflict resolution, peacemaking, and parenting. She is also the author of *Learning the Skills of Peacemaking* (Jalmar Press, 1995), *Peaceful Parents, Peaceful Kids* (Kensington, 2000), and *Hope and Healing: Peaceful Parenting in an Uncertain World* (Citadel, 2002). Naomi has been featured in magazines and newspapers and on radio and television. A former teacher, she served as a parenting expert for "Classroom Close-ups," an Emmy-winning public television show.

Naomi acts as a consultant to school districts, leads seminars, and runs parenting workshops. She headed the New Jersey State Bar Foundation's Conflict Resolution Advisory panel for eight years and taught public school for twenty-four years. She has worked with thousands of kids, parents, teachers, and administrators across the country for over twenty years. Her e-newsletter, *Peaceful Parents,* has broad international readership.

Her Web site, *www.learningpeace.com,* is a popular resource for those who want to create peace in their homes and schools. She has two grown sons and lives in New Jersey.

Other Great Books from Free Spirit

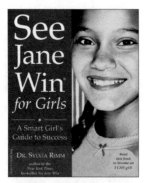

See Jane Win® for Girls
A Smart Girl's Guide to Success
by Dr. Sylvia Rimm
Dr. Rimm gives girls the "I Can" tips and tools they need to be confident, capable, eager to learn, and ready to lead. The experiences of successful women—from teachers, homemakers, and doctors to senators, scientists, and judges—inspire young readers; practical advice and encouragement helps them make positive changes and choices. Girls learn to win in all areas of life, from family and friends to school and learning, motivation, character development, and more. Includes quizzes and resources. For girls ages 9 & up.
$13.95; 128 pp.; softcover; illus.; 7" x 9"

You're Smarter Than You Think
A Kid's Guide to Multiple Intelligences
by Thomas Armstrong, Ph.D.
No longer are teachers asking about students, "How smart are they?" Instead, they're asking, "How are they smart?" In clear, simple language, this book introduces Howard Gardner's theory of multiple intelligences. Kids learn how they can use all eight intelligences in school, expand on them at home, and draw on them to plan for the future. Resources point the way to books, software, games, and organizations that can help kids develop the eight intelligences. Recommended for all kids, their parents, and educators. For ages 8–12.
$15.95; 192 pp.; softcover; illus.; 7" x 9"

What Do You Really Want?
How to Set a Goal and Go for It! A Guide for Teens
by Beverly K. Bachel with a special note from polar explorer Ann Bancroft
This book is a step-by-step guide to goal setting, written especially for teens. Each chapter includes fun, creative exercises, practical tips, words of wisdom from famous "goal-getters," real-life examples from teens, and success stories. Includes reproducibles. For ages 11 & up.
$12.95; 144 pp.; softcover; illus.; 6" x 9"

Stick Up for Yourself!
Every Kid's Guide to Personal Power and Positive Self-Esteem
Revised and Updated
by Gershen Kaufman, Ph.D., Lev Raphael, Ph.D., and Pamela Espeland
Simple text teaches assertiveness, responsibility, relationship skills, choice making, problem solving, and goal setting. For ages 8–12.
$11.95; 128 pp.; softcover; illus.; 6" x 9"

They Broke the Law—You Be the Judge
True Cases of Teen Crime
by Thomas A. Jacobs, J.D.
Judge Jacobs invites teens to preside over a variety of real-life cases. Readers learn each teen's background, the relevant facts, and the sentencing options available. After deciding on a sentence, they find out what really happened—and where each offender is today. Thought-provoking and eye-opening, this book is for all teens who want to know more about the juvenile justice system and the laws that pertain to them and their peers. For ages 12 & up.
$15.95; 224 pp.; softcover; 6" x 9"

Making the Most of Today
Daily Readings for Young People on Self-Awareness, Creativity, & Self-Esteem
by Pamela Espeland and Rosemary Wallner
Quotes from figures including Eeyore, Mariah Carey, and Dr. Martin Luther King Jr. guide you through a year of positive thinking, problem solving, and practical lifeskills—the keys to making the most of every day. For ages 11 & up.
$10.95; 392 pp.; softcover; 4¼" x 6¼"

Cliques, Phonies, & Other Baloney
by Trevor Romain
Written for every kid who has ever felt excluded or trapped by a clique, this book blends humor with practical advice as it tackles a serious subject. For ages 8–13.
$9.95; 136 pp.; softcover; illus.; 5⅛" x 7"

Bullies Are a Pain in the Brain
written and illustrated by Trevor Romain
Bullies are a pain in the brain—and every child needs to know what to do when confronted by one. This book combines humor with serious, practical suggestions for coping with bullies. For ages 8–13.
$9.95; 112 pp.; softcover; illus.; 5⅛" x 7"